EQUIPPE
to
EMERGE

The Distinctive Characteristics of Emerging Leaders...

YOMI ODUKOYA

Verbatim

Equipped To Emerge

Copyright © 2016 by Yomi Odukoya

Published by **Verbatim Communications Limited**
www.verbatimcomms.com
info@verbatimcomms.com
verbatimcommunications@yahoo.com
+234(0)8133602883, 07042178214

The views expressed in this book are those of the author and do not necessarily represent the views of the publishers.

ISBN: 978-978-52790-5-4

Printed and Bound in Nigeria

Contents

Dedication

To my darling wife Olutosin - for loving me, helping me, supporting my vision and believing in me; for insisting that I am much more than meets the eye. I love you more with each passing day.

To my daughter Fisola - for your infectious expectation of this work, for reading as it unfolded and for those fantastic cups of tea

To my son Fayokola - for your inner strength of character so admirable in a man so young, for asking insightful questions and checking up on me as I wrote

To my son Fadesayo - for your caring spirit, for treating me like the superhero of all daddies and for being such a joy to parent

Thank you for making me feel ten feet tall… I love you all

Acknowledgements

First, I give all glory to God - the Creator of the heavens and the earth for enabling me to start and complete this work.

I acknowledge my father, Justus Odukoya [of blessed memory] who raised me to be the man that I am, by being the example himself; my mother Deborah Odukoya for her undying love and many sacrifices that only mothers understand and my mother-in-law Comfort Orebiyi who is never short of a word of prayer for me. I acknowledge the love, support and prayers of my siblings – Kemi Olakanpo, Ayodele Odukoya and Babatunde Odukoya; Thank you for being there for me. I also acknowledge the love and support of Yemisi Lawson, Yewande Babayemi, Shola Balogun, Bibi Orebiyi and Michael Orebiyi. Thank you all.

The people who have served as my mentors, teachers or leaders over the years [directly or indirectly helping to nurture the seeds of greatness in me]; I acknowledge you all – with heartfelt gratitude. Rear Admiral Akinsola Johnson [rtd], Pastor Alfred Jegede, Bishop G.O. Fakeye [RIP], Prophet S.F. Korode, Pastor Kolade Adebayo-Oke, Mr. Deji Babayemi, Apostle M.D.A Oluwajoba, Pastor J-D Modede, Dr. Myles Munroe [RIP], Dr. Richard Pinder [RIP], Dr. Jerry Horner and Dr. David Burrows.

To my friends in the faith who have in one way or the other made my journey worthwhile, I salute you. Pastors Yomi & Stella Ekogbulu – thank you for receiving me. To the Youth Ministries of New Covenant Church [London] and Seal of Life Ministry [London], thank you for being a great part of this journey. To all the Pastors, Ministers and members of Christ United Ministries International [worldwide] – thank you for being a great family under a great vision. To the Youth Ministry of Christ United Ministries International Liberty House, Northampton – thank you for your support and love.

To my publisher – a wordsmith and teacher of the Word, Pastor Bidemi Mark-Mordi and her husband Pastor Mark Mordi – thank you both for your friendship, support and the great work done to make this a reality.

God bless you all.

Foreword

This work by Yomi Odukoya on Emerging Leadership is an excellent tool for the aspiring leader to obtain insight into the steps needed to emerge as a leader in a period where the number one deficit in the world is the deficit of leadership. His examination of the issues related to leadership as well as his examples and quotes from Moses to Muhammad Ali to Disney show his diverse understanding of leadership in both the secular and sacred realms which fulfils the leadership requirements of a true Kingdom Ambassador.

Yomi is one who understands how to be in the world, understand the world's system and yet lead beyond the wisdom of this world's system. Yomi is truly an example of an Emerging Leader. He has consistently shown this through his excellence in the corporate world as an executive and in the church world as a leader on several levels, including guiding younger leaders into their leadership destiny.

I highly recommend this work for all seeking to emerge as leaders with sound judgement and wisdom.

Dr. David Burrows
July 2016

Dr. Burrows is the Senior Pastor of Bahamas Faith Ministries International in Nassau, Bahamas. He is an internationally recognised speaker and also the author of many books and papers on youth, family, business, technology and leadership.

Preface

The word "emerge" is an interesting one. Coming from the Middle French word "émerger" and the Latin word "emergere", the word means "to rise out or up, bring forth or bring to light out of obscurity or concealment."

Emergence is an essential reality of human existence. From the day we emerge from the womb – an event usually celebrated as one of the wonders of nature, we join a cycle of continuous emergence from a variety of positions. For instance, each time we sleep, we emerge on the other side with new or continued responsibilities and challenges.

As we journey through life, we close the door on an achievement or "phase" of life and open the door, emerging into another. A child emerges into adolescence, the adolescent into adulthood. A pupil emerges from primary school into secondary school, college, university – and eventually into a chosen career path [where emergence continues from one project or task or achievement to the next].

When I initially put my heart into the vision of working with emerging leaders, I saw young leaders emerging into the big world of finance, relationships, marriage, careers, social responsibility, parenthood and spiritual development as the scope of what an emerging leader is. During my time spent serving this powerful class of leaders I discovered that all leaders emerge through a continuous exposure to life and its attendant challenges. Simply put, if you are a leader serving as an individual or as part of an organisation, you are an emerging leader so long as you remain relevant to your purpose.

I have studied many of the leaders who have changed or are changing the world, as we know it. Whether it is Gates in technology, Jordan in sports, Lincoln in politics, Merkel in politics, Parks in community development, Winfrey in entertainment or Munroe in Leadership, the one trait that is common to all these leaders is the pursuit of excellence. This pursuit is a never-ending one based on the realisation that the leader who will be excellent never actually arrives but remains on a quest. The pursuit of excellence ensures that a leader remains focused on his reason for being- purpose.

A wise teacher once likened the life of a leader to the peeling of an onion. As you peel off each layer, you discover more flavours. The paradox of course, is that the more you peel back each layer; the more your eyes also discover pain as they water from the layers being peeled back. With each layer that emerges, comes a new experience and challenge. You do have to peel each outer layer to get inside. Leaders - past and present, are usually able to share "layers" of experiences with us.

> Therefore, like the sun breaking through the clouds, leaders must emerge – complete with their inherent potential and varying capability for leadership.

Perhaps, natural law is our best pointer to the importance and relevance of emergence. Regardless of the differences in our culture, belief systems and social constructs, there is a universal acceptance of "day" which generally represents the period when the sun emerges [albeit briefly for some] and "night" which represents the period when the sky darkens. The 24-hour global financial system for instance, works around this law regulated by powers beyond the control of man. From the opening of markets in Asia to the closing of same markets in the Americas, the prices of stocks, commodities, derivatives, currencies as well as the viability of whole national economies are influenced.

As much as we may have learnt and given in service as leaders, there is yet so much more that is currently "concealed" in the future. The unlived portion of our existence as leaders is what this and the coming generations are waiting for. I, like many, believe that the best of me is yet to come. Therefore, like the sun breaking through the clouds, filling the sky with a breathtaking array of colours, bringing life, hope, energy, belief, motivation, power and renewal to our world - leaders must emerge – complete with their inherent potential and varying capability for leadership; consciously turn potential into power and put power through process to deliver the product of leadership – change.

Introduction

I t's day, night and day again. Monday, Wednesday and then Sunday ushers in the next Monday. It's January, June, then December and we start all over again. No one can remember when life started, no one knows who will be around when it ends. The continuum has in some way desensitised people to the value of time, and as such to the importance of assignments that need to be completed within boundaries. Leaders must continually emerge into this continuum to deliver on their assignments, impact their world and hand over the legacy baton to the next set.

There are times when we experience moments of absolute brilliance. Persons with exceptional skills and abilities emerge to light up the world with their gifts and serve their generation with distinction. Such leaders span a wide range of life areas – education, technology, science, arts, philosophy, finance, social service and many more. We want to hang on to these emerging leaders for as long as we can – telling of them to our children and they in turn to theirs. We dream of being like the "excellent ones" and nurture even more hopeful dreams of our children being so blessed.

Yet within the same continuum, we are witnesses to seasons of failure, misery, despondency and despair. Hard luck and desperation stories fill multiple newspaper columns; take up many pages on blogs as well as social media. People who would be leaders simply do not emerge, or as is often the case, become corrupted and derailed from purpose. Leadership therefore becomes the place where all news is bad news by default. People have learnt to live without good news. In this "vice-grip of darkness", people, communities and organisations lurch from one controversy to another, persons with political, religious and community-based authority "exposed" as frauds. There is a widening gap between reality and the great ideals that many yearn for. From this angle, all that can be seen is a "deep darkness" covering the land, and an even deeper darkness of "blissful ignorance" being displayed by people.

Somewhere between these two extremes, there is the vast land of the middle. This is the place where cups may be half-empty or half full [the emphasis being the "half"]. Generally, things are "okay". When people are asked *How are you doing today?* the

> **Leaders must emerge with sound character and integrity as the standard. The political, educational, community, financial, health and other governing systems of our world are waiting for the emergence and the manifestation of the true change makers.**

most common responses are *Not too bad* and *So-so*. To all intents and purposes, the leaders "exist" – but not a lot changes. There is just enough pain for it to be bearable, just enough work for people to survive, just enough good news to keep faint hopes alive and just enough bad news to deter people from dreaming of lofty achievements. People are comfortable with whatever cards they have been dealt by fate, life, Mother Nature or some other "blame-worthy" entity. There is a valid and well-used rationalisation for everything, such as, *"if it isn't broken, why fix it?"* or *"we are taking one day at a time"*.

I have spent time reflecting on change as a universal concept – examining the changes I have been through, those that have happened around me as well as those that have nothing to do with me. I have looked at the instigators of change, the drivers of change, the process of change, the obstacles to change, the beneficiaries of change as well as the victims of change. All these I find have something in common – a need for the right change to be delivered at the right time for the right reasons – and by the right persons.

This book focuses on the people who will instigate, drive, lead, plan, implement or champion change. Leaders must emerge with sound character and integrity as the standard. The political, educational, community, financial, health and other governing systems of our world are waiting for the emergence and the manifestation of the true change makers. Patient waiting has given way to an edgy expectation and in some cases, outright panic stations. In this book, we will examine who these emerging leaders are, what they should look like, think like, work like, behave like and live like.

As you go through the various sections and chapters of this book, you will perhaps find some qualities of the Emerging Leader described that you already possess and exhibit. You may also find other qualities that you have a challenge with. I hope this ignites a self-examination process within you where you ask yourself some or all of the following questions:

"If my world needs leaders, should I be one to step up?"
"Am I ready to emerge as the change that my generation requires?"
"If I do not emerge as a leader of change, who are we waiting for?"
"If no one steps up, what then?"

It is my belief that you will find enough to provoke you to desire the right change for this and the coming generations, and perhaps step up, step forward and present yourself for service that will bring the desired change to fruition.

Yomi Odukoya – June 2016

chapter 1

Timeless Imagination

"A man who has no imagination has no wings"
– Muhammad Ali

I t is often said that a person without vision will find leadership an impossible and unforgiving place to be. This is quite simply because leaders need to be persons who have seen something others have not seen, and have decided to point the way towards the realisation or implementation of that thing. Indeed, leaders differ in greatness by measure of how "real" the future they have seen is and how well they can relay it to followers to engender voluntary followership.

> **It is often said that a person without vision will find leadership an impossible and unforgiving place to be.**

There are many things a leader may possess that encourage followership – charisma, great ideas, communication skills, strength of character, empathy, emotional intelligence and the like. However, all of these great leadership tools serve to support the leader in delivering the version of utopia that they have seen. In other words, leaders with a hazy view of the solution they are meant to deliver will struggle to maintain self or others in the journey of delivery. This is why vision is seen as one of the most important attributes a leader must possess.

A great question to ask then is "where does vision come from?" I have been taught by many great leaders and have come to believe that **purpose is the origin of vision.** However, I would like to introduce to all Emerging Leaders reading this that there is a "data feed" for vision out there. There is a source regulated by purpose but not owned by purpose. This source consists of more data than any one person's purpose can manage. Let us examine this source of vision – **imagination.**

> **Imagination has no limits – indeed, it has the power to break a person free from the limitations of a current reality**

Think back through your growth as a person, professional or leader. You will probably remember times when you "looked into your future" and imagined great things or perhaps some not-so-great things. I remember as a child sometimes imagining my future as a football [soccer] player, and at other times imagining myself teaching large numbers of people in a really big venue. I never became a footballer, but I am now living the pictures I saw of being a teacher all those years ago.

> **Your imagination of potential solutions is what keeps the reality of a solution-driven future more real to you than the problem-ridden past or present.**

In fact, there are some of those pictures of a teacher I had as a child that I can almost match to actual experiences in the recent past. Imagination is so powerful that I dare to call it a form of time travel. Imagination is literally leaving the present to take in a view of a potential future.

Anyone can imagine anything. Imagination has no limits – indeed, it has the power to break a person free from the limitations of a current reality and allow that person to soar unfettered, uninhibited and with full access to a place of limitless possibilities. It is this awesome power of the imagination that makes it important

> **Imagination is not an event or a one-off activity. It is a fluid, ongoing examination of where you want to be.**

that a leader's purpose regulates his imagination. If purpose does not hold the regulatory power, leaders will spend all day dreaming and not enough time in the dissemination, planning, preparation, implementation and even celebration of the solution.

As an Emerging Leader you must continuously see something new for a better tomorrow, even as you implement what you saw yesterday, today. Your imagination of potential solutions is what keeps the reality of a solution-driven future more real to you than the problem-ridden past or present. As mentioned in the introduction, you are always "emerging" as a leader, so the requirement for a timeless and vivid imagination never becomes obsolete. It is dangerous for any leader to assume that they can "finish" emerging or outgrow any stage of emergence.

> **Creativity does not run where imagination is absent. Change is stymied in the absence of imagination.**

Imagination is not an event or a one-off activity. It is a fluid, ongoing examination of where you want to be. Each day, you make use of the "data" you've downloaded from your imagination of the future to build, re-build, update or alter the vision you have for yourself and those you are given the privilege to lead.

It is important that your vision keeps up with the trend and other changes around you, even those you have no impact or control on. For example, if you envision making a positive change to the way children are educated in primary schools by introducing more hands-on practical work, you will need to keep the picture you have updated with changes in technology that have happened as well as changes that are yet to occur, but are potentially part of another person's vision! Twenty years ago, "hands-on" probably referred to the use of pencils by students and chalk by teachers. Today, pencils and chalk have been largely replaced in classrooms by advanced technology.

> **Every product of a leader's imagination will be subjected to reactions.**

The story is often told of how Walt Disney's incredible imagination created what is today the world's premier holiday destination from a blank canvas – an expanse of land with nothing on it. With well over 130,000 visitors annually, the product of one man's imagination continues to have a major impact on how families across the world spend their holidays. The huge number of people employed by this organisation will also make a major contribution to local and national economies in the places where these parks are located.

Imagination is a tool that leaders cannot afford to ignore or misuse. Any leader who would be an agent of change must deploy this powerful tool effectively. Creativity does not run where imagination is absent. Change is stymied in the absence of imagination. Progress is an alien concept where imagination is ignored. As change agents, leaders need imagination to create things that do not exist as solutions to problems that do exist.

The five senses are quite useful to the emerging agent of change; however, it is the sixth and most powerful sense- imagination - that makes change happen. Leaders such as Martin Luther King, Rosa Parks and Nelson Mandela would no doubt have seen, heard, felt, smelt or tasted the effects of apartheid and racial segregation at different times. None of these experiences had the power to move them to lead their various struggles for freedom in the same way that their imagination of a better future could do.

The passion in Luther King's "I have A Dream" speech shows that his civil liberties fight had a grounding in something that he had explored to some detail in his mind. The speech starts from the description of experiences of segregation, justice and dignity but truly gains potency in the driving force of the "dream". His emphasis on "dream" in his speech is what moved many at the time and what most people remember about it today. The descriptive power in the words "red hills of Georgia", "table of brotherhood" and "four little children" shows that King had "seen" beyond what his physical sense of sight could deliver to him. Many of the things he described were viewed as impossible or highly unlikely at the time.

THE FOUR R's
As an Emerging Leader, you can measure the effectiveness of your imagination through the response of those who will be affected by the changes your ideas will bring. Every product of a leader's imagination [provided the idea is genuinely conceived with the

aim of creating something better than the status quo] will be subjected to the following reactions that I call the 4 R's.

Ridicule: Owing to the fact that imagination does not find its root in things that exist, it is quite possible that you will be a lone voice – or at best, one of a minority of voices – who can "see" the things you are proposing. Many will not be able to comprehend or make any sense of your idea and will default to the first line of defence – ridicule. Comments suggesting that strong substances have addled your mind will be quite common. Friends, professional colleagues and opponents of your ideas may all queue up to douse your idea in cold water – some with more bite than others. The "season of ridicule" is one where the emerging leader is required to be strong. It is this time of swimming against the current of accepted wisdom that marks out the great from the rest.

Reality-Blocking: Despite the understanding of the power of imagination, people are more likely to believe in the here and now – as the popular saying goes, *"seeing is believing"*. Reality-blocking is a common defence mechanism against the imagination of leaders. This is when people hit back at you with the facts of what can be seen in the physical. The biblical account of Moses leading the Israelites out of Egypt vividly illustrates this. Having gotten out of Egypt, against all odds, the Israelites encountered a barrier to progress - the Red Sea. They immediately lost faith in Moses' leadership and responded with recriminations, based on their reality.

> **As Emerging Leaders, we must learn in whatever position of influence we operate, to place the product of our imagination on the scales of integrity, accountability and justice.**

"and they said to Moses, "Is it because there are no graves in Egypt that you have taken us away to die in the desert? What in the world have you done to us by bringing us out of Egypt? Isn't this what we told you in Egypt, 'Leave us alone so that we can serve the Egyptians, because it is better for us to serve the Egyptians than to die in the desert'?"
(Exodus 14: 11-12)

Obviously, these people did not really want to remain in slavery, neither did they want to die. Reality-blocking picks out what the troubled mind instantly perceives as the option of "least discomfort".

Resistance: This is an ever-present reaction to change which starts as early as the conception [imagination] of the change. You will probably get told in many ways how your idea will not work. You may experience denial

> **Your challenge as an Emerging Leader is to free your imagination to unlock solutions for the problems that exist today – even for the problems we are yet to discover.**

with the people and resources you require to make the idea. Any support you receive for the idea or project may also be perfunctory or reluctantly given. It is quite possible that the resistance will come from the same people you are expecting to champion your course. Some resistance will be overt and in your face, others will be cleverly covert but equally as strong. Even the optimists you know may sound more pessimistic about your idea than you expect the pessimists to.

It is important as an emerging leader that you understand the drivers of this resistance. In all likelihood, the product of your imagination will lead to a change that will affect people directly or indirectly. Resistance is often driven by:

Fear of leaving the security of familiarity in favour of the unknown – People are by design creatures of habit, preferring the known above the discomfort of what could be.

> *"People have a hard time letting go of their suffering. Out of a fear of the unknown, they prefer suffering that is familiar"* - Thich Nhat Hanh

Fear of believing in what could eventually fail – With each failed attempt to produce the light bulb, there would have been a steady decrease in the numbers of those who stood with Thomas Edison and an increase in those who resisted his ideas. It can be quite a challenge to continue championing a cause that most knowledgeable people believe will be a spectacular failure.

Fear of the impact of change in the event of success– People will weigh up the perceived pros and cons of living in a world that contains the product of your imagination. *Will this new technology lead to easier production of food? On the other hand, will it lead to members of our family losing their jobs in the food processing plant?* Those who value the manual jobs above the "unproven" productivity improvements will resist your ideas.

Reluctant Respect: Having ridden the gauntlet through ridicule, reality-blocking and resistance, the product of your imagination –

if you still believe it – starts to garner the reluctant respect of those who already "killed" your idea but are surprised to find it still standing and going strong. This is the point where the product of your imagination changes how people perceive you. You then move away from "flawed genius" to a "respected thinker". Your social network popularity soars and many are now willing to discuss the assistance they offered you during your journey to the top.

It will be amiss of me not to sound a note of warning regarding the dangers of imagination. The imagination of a person who lacks integrity or whose personality has been formed by a history of negative influences can be quite dangerous. The Second World War came into being largely due to the imagination of Adolf Hitler. He envisioned a world subservient to a superior German race. And today, severe acts of terrorism are still being inflicted on our world – the products of imagination steeped in hatred, confusion and misguided loyalty. There are nations across the world whose governments enact and empower laws that have no backing in natural law and subject portions of their populace to persecution – again, the product of imagination. As Emerging Leaders, we must learn in whatever position of influence we operate, to place the product of our imagination on the scales of integrity, accountability and justice.

You should continuously ask yourself these five questions as you apply the power of imagination to the delivery of your purpose:

1. Will or can the product of my imagination serve or help to improve humanity?

2. Is my imagination subject to the governance of integrity?
3. Is my imagination subject to the governance of accountability?
4. How will my world deal with the impact of the product of my imagination?
5. Will I be happy to be the "impacted party" if someone else imagined this?

Your challenge as an Emerging Leader is to free your imagination to unlock solutions for the problems that exist today – even for the problems we are yet to discover. If anyone can, you can.

Examine - Equip - Emerge

Timeless Imagination

1. Imagination is about visiting the future and bringing back with you the vision of the solution to the problems of today. As a leader, what vision of a better tomorrow have you seen and brought back to implement today?

   ....
   ....
   ....
   ....
   ....

2. What work have you done (or are you currently doing) with any vision you have seen of the future? (In other words, is your imagination producing results)?

   ....
   ....
   ....
   ....
   ....

3. What obstacles or hurdles have you faced (physically or mentally) when you imagine yourself delivering great value to your family, community, or workplace?

   ....
   ....
   ....

....

....

4. How have you dealt with opposition to the ideas you have brought from your imagination? (Sharing with a coach is usually a good strategy if you find yourself facing difficult opposition).

....

....

....

....

....

5. What experience have you had of the FOUR Reactions that people can have towards your imagination?

....

....

....

....

....

Let us wrap up this discussion with three simple tasks you can do to exercise your imaginative powers.

6. Imagine yourself doing something important to you that you do not currently have the ability to do. What changes would you need to undergo in order to get there?

....

....

....

....

....

7. Imagine you have a blank canvas to redesign your home [any design you come up with will be built for free, so money is no object]. What would be in the new house? What would not be in it? Why would you have anything you imagine?

....

....

....

....

....

8. Imagine yourself as the leader of your community, organisation or nation for 100 days free. What is the first thing you would change that will benefit others?

....

....

....

....

....

.

"I think leadership's always been about two main things, imagination and courage" – Paul Keaton

chapter 2

Perceptive Insight

"Nothing is more terrible than activity without insight."

- Thomas Carlyle

M any who have attended my seminars have asked whether leadership has to do with a "hands-off" or generic view of management. Each time, I have provided the simple response that leadership is neither a generic activity nor a "higher management" position of overseeing the detailed management performed by others. Leadership is about delivering positive change to specific situations, providing otherwise unavailable solutions to specific questions and adding value to specific areas of assignment and motivating people to move in a specific direction. All these "specifics" require a key component of the leader's toolkit – insight.

> **Insight comes with a level of detail that enables the leader stay ahead of the pack with regards to problem solving.**

Insight is the leader's capacity to secure a profound and accurate understanding of a situation, problem, idea, concept, subject or person. Insight is much deeper than "knowing about" or "knowing of" something. For instance, if as a leader, you find yourself dealing with a problematic situation, insight represents your ability to get to the root of the matter, thereby making it possible for you to emerge

> **A leader does not instinctively catch insight; rather, insight is developed as a result of extensive investment over time into a variety of problems, dissecting issues into their component parts and understanding the visible and invisible relationships between stakeholders.**

with a strategy or plan that best resolves the problem. Your insight as a leader enables you to comprehend the "full weight" of a situation including what it is, why it came to be and how the situation affects people, systems and organisations in the short, medium and long term. Insight also gives you a view of the various paths that will not lead to a solution, those that will lead to a partial solution and those that will lead to a permanent solution [if available]. In other words, insight is more than the discovery of a solution or an "eureka" moment. Insight comes with a level of detail that enables the leader stay ahead of the pack with regards to problem solving.

The wrong approach is to view insight as a "gift" that is manifested by certain leaders – or some "soft skill" that comes naturally to a selected band of people. This is because insightful leaders appear to pull out solutions from some dark place where most linear thinkers have not been. However, this cannot be farther from the truth. A leader does not instinctively catch insight; rather, insight is developed as a result of extensive investment over time into a variety of problems, dissecting issues into their component parts and understanding the visible and invisible

> **It is pertinent to say that if you do not have deep insight into yourself, you will never emerge as an effective leader.**

relationships between stakeholders. As leaders do this more often, they emerge from each situation as more powerful users of their thinking and comprehension muscles.

As an Emerging Leader the first level of insight you need is **self-insight**. This is primarily because leadership is about giving of yourself. Over your leadership career you will give your time, resources, knowledge, ability, as well as your physical, mental and emotional strength to the people, communities and organisations you lead. It is therefore pertinent to say that if you do not have deep insight into yourself, you will never emerge as an effective leader. Your self-insight is akin to a full-scale scan of all you have in your armoury, and how much you have of each item to give as a leader. No one can know you better than you do.

Let's say for example you are looking to develop a mentorship programme for young ex-offenders. A lot of importance will rightly be attached to doing the groundwork with the correctional authorities, preparing the educational materials, getting the required training in youth coaching, getting the required licenses to operate within the prison services and getting the right level of financial support. However, a major key to the success or failure of your programme will be the internal drivers that "released" this vision from within you. How much empathy do you have for young persons who may have been damaged by gruelling home situations as well as time spent in prison? How much patience have you developed to handle the few participants who will throw your help back in your face? What do you know about your ability to work with intransigent correctional facility workers who may believe that your programme is a whole load of empty words?

I once listened to elite soldiers [Marines] share with prospective enlisters about what it takes to be successful in the Corps. As expected, there was a lot shared about supreme fitness and strength – stressing the ability to do a set number of crunches, pull-ups, press-ups and run a set distance all in a ridiculously short space of time. Others talked about obeying every order given as one of the keys to success. Being a team player is also high on the list – elite soldiers never work as individuals, the team is always bigger. However, the one success key mentioned that applies from the first day of boot camp to the day the elite soldier is discharged is what one Marine described as "knowing all of yourself, especially that you really want to be a Marine". The soldier went on to explain that the same training is given to all members but at the end of the day, it is the person who was trained [not the training in itself] that will have to overcome the challenges that a Marine faces. Paraphrasing his words, "You must know who you are; you must know that you want to be a Marine; you must know why you want to be a Marine; you must believe on the first day that you are already a Marine – then you are on your way".

> **If you want to achieve anything as a leader, you must invest time and energy in understanding what makes a variety of stake-holders tick.**

Second to self-insight, the emerging leader needs to develop what I will call "**subject-matter insight**". This is a deep-rooted understanding of the area of assignment in which you are emerging into relevance and leadership. It makes sense for a political leader to develop political insight, just as it makes sense for a leader in the world of sports to develop insight in his or her chosen area of assignment. There is no more pitiful disaster than the would-be leader whose understanding of relevant subjects is suspect or entirely shallow.

As a leader emerging into your area of assignment, you will need to invest time and effort into the pursuit and acquisition of knowledge. The acquisition of knowledge is however just the appetiser. With an untold amount of information available electronically, pretty much anyone with access to the internet can seek and find knowledge on any subject. For your knowledge drive to become an insight quest, you will need to have an insatiable desire to keep uncovering more about the subject area. You will also need a determination to overcome the "dead ends" that you will no doubt come across in your insight quest – and you will need discipline to stay on track, not getting distracted from your quest. We will talk about these "three D's" in a later chapter.

One key advantage of acquiring subject matter insight is the confidence it generates in the Emerging Leader. When you are armed with a detailed knowledge of your subject matter and you come in contact with people, this confidence enhances your scope of impact. The confidence is almost tangible – so much that there is an increased expectation - from the people you meet – of a positive experience with you.

A long time ago, in Lagos, Nigeria, I came across a young man simply referred to as "Jo-Jo" by his mates. At the time, he was 20 years old and had spent 8 years working as a "roadside mechanic".

He had spent the first 4 years as an apprentice in the same establishment. I was there with a friend who had taken his car in for a quick check up. As soon as we stated our business, two other youngsters were dispatched in search of Jo-Jo. See, my friend's car was an expensive one; and Jo-Jo had a growing reputation for his deep study and love for such cars. None of the other mechanics felt comfortable enough to discuss the problems this expensive car might have – and my friend was certainly not ready to discuss it with any of them. A few minutes later Jo-Jo walked in, carrying with him that "air" of confidence that comes with subject-matter insight. He spoke about the car with an ease that belied his youth but was the evidence of his growing leadership in his profession. He may not have been the most educated man around, and he may not even have been the best "uneducated mechanic" around; however, his insight into a particular subject set him apart from the crowd.

> **As an Emerging Leader, you will be challenged to affect your world using uncommon knowledge and information not yet known to the majority.**

> **Not only do you have to possess deep insight into what gives today, you also have to be perceptive enough to sense the changes in the terrain you have committed to serve in, even before these changes come into being.**

The third level of insight an emerging leader must possess is the "stakeholder insight". This involves having an in-depth appreciation of the individuals, groups, teams, organisations and communities that are relevant to the leader or his work. If you want to achieve anything as a leader, you must invest time and energy in understanding what makes a variety of stake-holders tick. Whatever area you aspire to lead in, there will always be a wide spectrum of stakeholders. Some of the stakeholders will be those who require your services, feed input into your service delivery or perhaps use your output to do their "thing".

From 2008 to 2012, I was a primary school governor in Northamptonshire, UK. I saw firsthand how teachers had to understand the needs of the pupils, school and the parents who required their services. They also had to understand the curriculum that provided input for their service [lessons had to be taught from specific content and to specified standards]. To cap it off, they also had to provide a load of data as output to the school governors and Local Education Authority who used such output to determine the effectiveness of teaching services. Finally, there were "stakeholders" who did not interact with the teacher at all – political observers, journalists and the like – who took interest in the services of teachers from a distance. Back then, teachers were those who, in addition to their internally-driven desire to succeed, were able to find a balance to serve their stakeholders based on their in-depth knowledge of the stakeholders' needs.

Now, imagine your organisation or community is depending on you to propose a solution to an existing problem in an area your knowledge is deeply respected. So far, my experience with leaders at various levels affirms that in addition to the insight you have on the subject-matter, you must clearly identify key stakeholders, gain insight into their needs and positional views of the problem you intend to resolve. Ignorance or inadequate knowledge of stakeholders can stifle the progress or render completely redundant, the work of a leader.

We often read of highly effective and influential leaders [Dr. Nelson Mandela is one of such I have studied] and appreciate the way they set about changing their worlds. I firmly believe that it took great insight into the people that he was working or fighting for, as well as those he was "fighting" against for him to achieve the feat he did.

The value and impact of stakeholder insight is all around us today. It is the insight that sales managers must seek into their intended sales targets; the insight that political leaders must seek into their constituents and voting public; the insight that teachers and youth leaders need to catch concerning the mind-set of young persons. Indeed, if you believe – like I do that a husband or wife is one of the key stakeholders in a marriage, then you will agree that this level of insight is required as one of the building blocks of a successful marriage.

Notice that I have branded this section "**perceptive** insight". As an Emerging Leader, it is not just the depth of insight you have that will enable you stand out from the crowd; it is how that insight leads you into action that makes the ultimate difference. Perception [from the Latin word "*percipere*" which means "to obtain or to gather"] is a quality that is manifested in action and acknowledged by the quality of result that the leader produces through that action. By using the word "perceptive" to qualify insight, I am talking about leaders who raise the bar – having insight into what others are yet to see or understand. As an

Emerging Leader, you will be challenged to affect your world using uncommon knowledge and information not yet known to the majority.

It is also crucial to note that in a world that is as dynamic as the one we live in today; knowledge is not static. What we considered current information yesterday will in all probability show up on the list of obsolete information tomorrow. This adds a challenging dimension to the leadership quality of perceptive insight. Not only do you have to possess deep insight into what gives today, you also have to be perceptive enough to sense the changes in the terrain you have committed to serve in, even before these changes come into being. The greatest traders are those who sense the mood swings and volatility of the markets – and can anticipate the most likely responses of market participants to these fluctuations. The great golfers like Tiger Woods, Jack Nicklaus and Severiano Ballesteros were able to combine their confidence in their own skill and capabilities with an appreciation of what the conditions were expected to be on the given day of play – and still deliver great shots with a flexibility that put both aside in favour of what parameters changed in the few seconds before the shot was taken. Perceptive insight is nimble, agile and yet focused enough to make use of minute details in the delivery of effective leadership.

> **Your challenge as an Emerging Leader is not to be the smartest kid on the block, but the keenest learner, thereby ensuring that you never get stale.**

I remember studying languages such as ADA, C and C++ during my degree programme in Computing at the London South Bank

University. A few years down the line, these languages have been aggressively pushed out of relevance by various incarnations of Java and a host of newer, more user-friendly coding languages. Coding standards have also moved on in response to the new languages. The almost unstoppable charge of globalisation also ensured that end-user computing requirements changed rapidly, bringing with it a new, more informed and internationally connected class of users - further changing the software development terrain. In order to remain relevant in this area, software engineers are constantly on a learning drive. The age of "computing experts" is gone, now to be replaced by different specialities, which enable professionals to develop the levels of insight that can make them leaders in their chosen fields.

KNOWLEDGE BEGETS INSIGHTS

To develop any or all of these levels of insight, the starting point is always knowledge [that you either have or do not have]. This knowledge can be classified based on the following:
1. Open-Open
2. Open-Closed
3. Closed-Open
4. Closed-Closed

The "**Open-Open**" knowledgebase is the knowledge you have about a problem or situation that other people also have access to [typically, what is in the public domain]. This will be the most accessible data or information available e.g. the minutes of an Annual General Meeting or the contents of a policy document. The ease of access to this information makes it the minimum knowledge base that you should have as an emerging leader. This information in itself will not constitute "insight" but will be foundational and essential to problem solving. Your skill of discernment will be tested by the availability and sheer "volume" of this knowledgebase. As an emerging leader, you should ask yourself the following:

1. Am I missing any openly available information?
2. Do I know where to find the openly available information?
3. How do I acquire any openly available information that I do not have yet?

The "**Open-Closed**" knowledgebase is what you have access to [or have expertise in] that other stakeholders do not have e.g. the results of some analysis you have conducted or some technical information entrusted to you by reason of your position or role. This could be the type of knowledge that made your organisation select you as the prime candidate to solve a problem. As this may not be readily available information, it is quite likely to be confidential in nature or of such sensitivity that it requires careful handling. It may even be so sensitive that it becomes unusable in problem solving. Nevertheless, this knowledge you have is a key building block of your insight into the matter at hand. Your discretion and sensitivity will be tested by the exclusive nature of this knowledgebase. The following questions may be provoked as you examine this level of knowledge:

· What uncommon knowledge do I have access to?
· Is it lawful to use this information to resolve a particular problem?
· How can I leverage this knowledge in relation to this problem?

The "**Closed-Open**" knowledgebase is what you do not have

access to or expertise in that other stakeholders may well have e.g. classified information that excludes you from access by virtue of your role or a "non-disclosure agreement". It is typically difficult to ascertain the importance of this information to a particular situation until it becomes necessary to access or use it. Dealing with this knowledgebase tests your collaboration and interpersonal skills as you may need more than one stakeholder to help you "complete a picture". As an emerging leader entrusted with solution delivery, you should ask the following questions:

- What important knowledge do I lack that others have?
- Do I require some "hidden" knowledge in order to serve effectively?
- Which relationships need to be built or sustained to ensure the flow of essential information into my delivery?

The **Closed-Closed** knowledgebase refers to information or data that you do not have, and no one appears to have access to. In some instances, you know the information is out there, but neither you nor anyone in your network can get a hold of it. In other instance, you are perhaps not aware of the existence of this information. Your interrogation, research and analytical skills will be sorely tested by the drive to discover.

The difficulty with this knowledgebase is in getting to a position where you can confirm or deny its existence, validity or importance. As competitive as business and politics are, the game of "bluff and counter-bluff" is often played, with one opponent unsure of the information held by the other, and vice-versa. In a well-known organisation I once worked for, the senior management internally admitted that competitive advantage depends on service delivery, and not just service availability.

Typical questions an emerging leader should ask in this position include:

- Is there any information out there that we do not have?
- How can we access information that we can neither define nor ignore?
- Is the real value in searching, or in using what we already have?

Insight is a key distinguishing attribute of the emerging leader. In closing this chapter, I advise that insight should not be confused with "experience". Even the least experienced workers on a team can speak insightfully if they are willing to invest time (life) in building information into understood knowledge. They must also be willing to apply what they understand – learning from every mistake made along the way.

Your challenge as an Emerging Leader is not to be the smartest kid on the block, but the keenest learner, thereby ensuring that you never get stale. More value is added to our world by those who learn than by those who know.

Examine - Equip - Emerge

Perceptive Insight

1. "Insight is the leader's ability to obtain a profound and accurate understanding of a situation, problem, idea, concept, subject or person." How important has insight been to you in your journey as a leader?

    ....
    ....
    ....
    ....
    ....

2. Self-insight is the in depth knowledge of the value you carry within you and how this value can benefit the world around you. What are the top 5 things you know about yourself that can show the emerging leader in you?

    ....
    ....
    ....
    ....
    ....

3. Subject matter insight is the profound knowledge of your chosen area of work or influence. In your area of work please identify and list what you need to have deep insight of in order to be effective as a leader?

    ....
    ....

....

....

....

4. Stakeholder insight is the in depth understanding of the individuals, teams and groups that affect you or are affected by your work as an emerging leader. Describe the role your knowledge of people has played in your leadership career.

....

....

....

....

....

5. Perceptive insight is nimble, agile and yet focused enough to make use of minute details in the delivery of excellent leadership. Can you think of examples where you have been flexible enough - and yet grounded enough - to make the best use of what you know?

....

....

....

....

....

6. More value has been added to our world by those who lean than by those who know. Please look into the last 6 months of your life and detail out the increase in knowledge you have gained through learning.

....

....

....

....

....

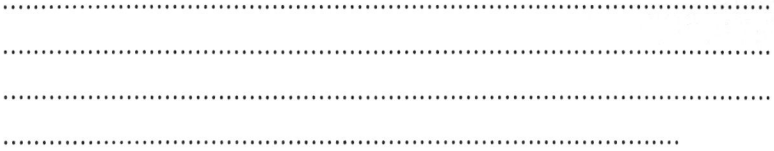

"In today's complex and fast-moving world, what we need even more than foresight or hindsight is insight"
– Napoleon Bonaparte

chapter 3

Authenticity & Integrity

"Honesty and integrity are absolutely essential for success in life - all areas of life".
– Zig Ziglar

Many years ago as a child, I watched a popular television programme "*Sesame Street,*" which used a series of cartoon clips as educational tools for children. Something from a particular episode still makes me smile when I remember it. In this episode, as a way of showing children that the word "Egg" starts with an "E," a cow incubates an egg laid by a chicken. Eventually, the egg hatches and produces a chicken (what else?). The surprise factor hits home when the young chicken opens its beak and utters the sound, "Moo!"

There are many reasons this clip would stick in the memory including the odd sight of a cow incubating a chicken's egg and the fact that the egg somehow remained unbroken through that ordeal. However, what makes this really interesting is the sound made by the newly-hatched chick. The natural chirping sound appeared to have been influenced by who incubated the egg – and not by who the chick really was. In the same way, many emerging leaders are conditioned by external influences to be something or someone else.

As you rise in leadership, people's expectations of you increase. Every group you serve or interact with will have an expectation of your leadership or service. This more than anything else is what leadership scholars have called the "burden of leadership". It is not so much the difficulty of your particular terrain that makes leadership a complex, demanding and challenging occupation. It is the fact that leadership is more about who you are than what you do.

> **From leaders in government, to those in business or the community, no one is exempt from the pressure of expectation and delivery.**

There is indeed a great weight of expectation that comes with leadership and many have buckled under that weight. From leaders in government, to those in business or the community, no one is exempt from the pressure of expectation and delivery. Ordinarily, this expectation should be what inspires and galvanizes leaders, making them even more effective. The reality, though, is that many persons in positions of leadership [formal and informal] have not discovered enough about themselves to handle the expectation. When a leader is not really sure of his or her identity, there is a tendency to act out the people's expectations in order to receive praise, positive feedback, promotions, re-election or some other benefit. This is, unfortunately for some, the place where authenticity is sacrificed for personal convenience or benefit.

> **It is however crucial that none of these should result in the Emerging Leaders becoming clones or replicas of anyone they are looking up to.**

Authenticity as a requirement for sound leadership is not a new concept. The concept and its attendant manifestations have been defined many times over by leadership scholars and practitioners. I recall a simple phrase that formed a constant part of the advice my father gave me, especially when I was leaving home for college. **"Be yourself all the time"** he would say. As a young man, I took those words of advice seriously. The message was clear: "do not try to be anybody else – be real, be authentic, be you!" This was a key message for my development.

First, I had to discover what "yourself" stood for in that context. There was no way I could remember to be what I did not know – so I did a lot of soul-searching and self-analysis – with the result that I became quite self-aware even at a young age. **Self-awareness is a core component of authenticity.** It is the basis from which the "real you" is launched; it also serves as a correctional voice whenever you exhibit a character trait that is not true to the "real you".

It is important for Emerging Leaders to be given a healthy dose of mentorship, counselling, advice, training and other assistance geared towards developing them to be the best leaders possible. It is however crucial that none of these should result in the Emerging Leaders becoming clones or replicas of anyone they are looking up to.

> **Discovering who you are is not a one-off activity. It is an on-going process that starts from your childhood, through adolescence and into adulthood. I believe that all leaders must have a lifetime commitment to self-discovery.**

A lot of times, I have seen lots of young men and women stray from the path of leadership relevance by opting to become photocopies of another leader – in speech. I have also seen more "mature" leaders attempt to "re-define" themselves (after a period of flat lining in their career) and get it all wrong. Copying is the result of a loss of leadership identity, the evidence of a loss in confidence and the beginning of a slide away from significance into insignificance. Clients and colleagues will simply wonder why they need to listen to the "copy" when they can get more from the "original".

So, what then is authentic leadership? This is simply *serving out of your true identity, your true values, your true experience, your true history, your true learning, your true passion and your true character to others in the delivery of your purpose.* You are not born as an authentic leader – your authenticity arises from who you have become through your life and learning. As I have mentioned in many teaching sessions, everyone is born with inherent leadership ability – the crux of the matter is: how many people actually discover enough about themselves to develop and deploy those abilities.

Discovering who you are is not a one-off activity. It is an on-going process that starts from your childhood, through adolescence and into adulthood. I believe that all leaders must have a lifetime commitment to self-discovery. If you cannot learn from yourself, there is little chance you will learn from any other. Your specific experiences of life have an uncanny way of shaping the way you understand and react to a variety of situations as you proceed through life.

One of the leaders who served as a mentor to me in my youth told the story of how his difficult upbringing shaped his decisions and formed his outlook on life and leadership. Having been brought up by a single parent [his mother] in an extremely violent neighbourhood, he survived gang-induced fights, numerous prison sentences for a variety of misdemeanours and extreme poverty to find his way into university, and eventually the church where he now serves as a pastor to many whose early

> An important process to the development of your authenticity as a leader is having your deeply held values severely tested or put under pressure either from external or internal forces. Much like faith, your values become stronger and more entrenched with each "test" that they successfully navigate.

lives are a repetition of his life's pattern. Once when asked how he is able to affect the lives of so many young people who are living violent lives and living in violent areas, he said, "I show them who I am – warts, bruises and all – and they respond knowing that I come to them with a true and genuine desire to help." This is authentic leadership. When people realise that you have been to where they are trying to go, they will follow you. They will listen to you.

Authentic leadership is living out your values as a person in your area of assignment. These values will have a major impact on the type of leader you become. Understanding the values that you hold as precious is key to self-

> Leaders have a decisive influence in shaping the culture of the organisation within which they operate.

awareness and self-discovery. Therefore, understanding your values is key to your authenticity as a leader. The values you uphold will effectively drive what you permit and what you forbid as a person and a leader. These values work on the inside to shape what people see of you on the outside.

As an emerging leader with One-2-One [now a part of the telecommunications giant "T-Mobile"], I worked in a team led by a senior manager, Mr. Dobson. This gentleman was one of those who confirmed to me what type of leader I would become. I have always valued respect as an important cog of leadership. This is one of the core values that I live by. On a particular project, my co-worker and I overlooked an important checkpoint, which could have been quite costly. The next day, as we were being berated for this oversight by another senior executive, Mr. Dobson walked in. He spoke a few words to calm the irate executive down and then proceeded to do what I believed the senior executive should have done – asking what went wrong, establishing areas of improvement and not labelling us by our shortcomings. I truly appreciated the personal respect accorded me – and much later, I discovered that respect was a key value that Mr. Dobson lived by. I have since moved on as a manager

> **The key message here for all leaders – emerging and established – is you should not "grow out of yourself." In all of your growth and development, there should only be one version of you – and that is the real you!**

> **The leader with integrity will not speak or act in any way that is at odds with his or her values or beliefs.**

and leader, never allowing the priority, severity, importance or urgency of a project, to determine the level of respect I give to my colleagues and clients. I also have a strong resolve not to let external stimuli influence the quality of delivery of my service.

An important process to the development of your authenticity as a leader is having your deeply held values severely tested or put under pressure either from external or internal forces. Much like faith, your values become stronger and more entrenched with each "test" that they successfully navigate.

> **As an Emerging Leader, you will be faced on a regular basis – typically many times in a single day, with choices and decisions to make.**

I have heard many scholars describe authenticity as "calling things as you see them" – being as blunt in speech as you feel about a situation or person. Whilst there is some merit to this argument, it is often one that misleads leaders and allows them to slip into the common error of only hearing themselves think and speak.

I recently worked with an organisation in Europe where the prevailing culture [that many senior managers were proud of] was one of "challenging" deficient behaviour or results. Challenging deficient behaviour

> **Integrity is staying on track with a high moral standard even when conventional or accepted norms would tolerate a slip in standards. Integrity is doing the right thing at the right time, with the right people, for the right reasons, every time.**

can, if properly implemented, be a culture that promotes effective working and positive behaviour. In this instance though, the "alpha-leader" within a core function of the bank had a tough-talking, take-no-prisoners reputation, with a tendency to quickly move from disarming calmness to incandescent rage. In barely veiled attempts to gain the approval of this "alpha-leader," many managers within the group sought to outdo each other in the level of rudeness, disrespect and foul language that they could muster. Shouting down people at meetings and playing "tough" to the gallery became all too common. It was not unusual to witness deliberate attempts to embarrass a colleague during team meetings. Effectively, there were too

> **The greatest problem your integrity is likely to face is the rationalisation that has become endemic in today's society.**

many attempted clones of the "alpha-leader." The consequences of this unauthentic behaviour amongst leaders included project delivery inertia, unusually high turnover and low morale amongst the middle managers and supervisors, which in due course spread to various teams. The key lesson I picked up from this experience is that leaders have a decisive influence in shaping the culture of the organisation within which they operate. However, while emerging leaders should be encouraged to learn from the established leaders, it is important that the established leader's influence does not create a "groupie" following of workers whose quest to "be like the boss" overshadows their natural growth into leaders.

To be clear, growth and improvement are natural processes in leaders. It is pertinent to note that whatever lives but stops growing starts dying. Therefore, the call for authenticity is not one that shuts out the need for growth. The key message here for all leaders – emerging and established – is you should not "grow out of yourself." In all of your growth and development, there should only be one version of you – and that is the real you! The real you is the value-creating, change-delivering leader that your family, community, organisation, country and generation have been waiting for. The real you is the embodiment of your purpose and your value to the clients, colleagues and friends that you will impact. The real you is the unique entity that no one else can successfully replace. The real you is the one that is fully aware of the responsibility to be you and is fully committed to delivering on that responsibility. The real you is the authentic you!

> "It takes years to define your values, set moral standards to live by, build a reputation for integrity and develop the character to sustain that reputation… it however takes one minute of an indiscretion or a slight lowering of the standards you set for yourself to lose it all. Once you have lost the integrity platform, you lose the respect, honour and trust that came with it. And when you lose them, it is at least twice as difficult to reclaim them."

Integrity

Integrity in a leader is quite closely related to authenticity. It is difficult to imagine a leader who has one but not the other. I will go as far as saying that you either have both authenticity and integrity or you have neither. As to which one comes first, that is a "chicken-egg" issue that we will not discuss here.

Integrity is that position a leader takes where adherence to sound moral and ethical principles is natural and continuous. Integrity is much more than obedience to laws and rules; it is much more than the appearance of good behaviour; it is much more than telling the truth. Integrity [from the root Latin word "integer"] describes a consistency and congruence between the various aspects of the leader – including espoused values and beliefs, actions, reactions and general behaviour. The leader with integrity will not speak or act in any way that is at odds with his or her values or beliefs.

As an Emerging Leader, you will be faced on a regular basis – typically many times in a single day, with choices and decisions to make. Some decisions will be of the "no-brainer" category, while others will be more difficult to make. Of those that are difficult, there will be choices between "right and wrong". In some cases, there will be the "grey-area temptation".

In the early nineties, I was told the true story of a Human Resources Manager in a government organisation in West Africa. During a time of difficulty for this country, jobs for graduates were a very scarce commodity. A person with a First Class grade in degree examinations coupled with a recommendation from the university authorities would struggle to get an entry-level job – because of the economic misfortunes that had befallen the country. One afternoon, an elderly man came to the HR Manager's office with his son who badly needed a job. There was one role vacant but the education and experience that this man's son had did not fit the profile required for the job. The HR Manager duly said to the elderly man, *"Sir, we appreciate your son's application and we will keep his CV on record, but we cannot take this application any further today."* At this point the elderly man placed an envelope on the table and said *"This is for you sir – ten thousand dollars, in cash … just to process the application – and there is more if you can influence the decision in favour of my boy."* The HR Manager who did not earn up to ten thousand dollars in a year looked at the envelope, the young man and finally quite intently at the elderly man. *"I'm truly sorry sir, as I said; we cannot take this application any further on this occasion. Please take your money and leave."*

Integrity is doing the right thing even when no one will know that you did. Integrity is staying on track with a high moral standard even when conventional or accepted norms would tolerate a slip in standards. Integrity is doing the right thing at the right time, with the right people, for the right reasons, every time. In the preceding story, the HR Manager knew that if he took the bribe (or "encouragement" as it was called in his culture), he would have solved a few of his financial problems. He also knew that no one outside of that room would know about the bribe. Crucially, he knew that even if no one else was aware of the bribe, he would have dropped his standards of integrity and compromised his own values as well as those of the organisation. He also knew that any advice he would give his children about integrity would at best be hypocritical, and at worst, insincere.

Integrity does not compromise or take the "grey-area" route. The greatest problem your integrity is likely to face is the rationalisation that has become endemic in today's society. Gone are the days of absolute truth and falsehood. Gone are the days when laws drew a line between right and wrong. As you may be aware, we live in a world where people are encouraged to define their own "truth." In today's world, the young grow with the notion that in life, the end justifies the means. Acceptability has been extended to various activities through rationalisation. Illegal activities have been downgraded to "misdemeanours" and "indiscretions." Politicians, in a bid to win as many votes as possible have failed to uphold truth, morality and ethical behaviour. As an Emerging Leader though, you do have a choice to make. Will you accept the stripping away of sound values and ethics in order to get ahead in life, or will you define and stick to your values and high standards, regardless of the peer, managerial and community pressure that you face?

Before we start to think that the issue of integrity is only limited to the political class or the management of investment banks and such organisations, please consider the following examples – some of which may hit close to home.

- An applicant for a Test Manager role overstates his earnings in his last job in order to set a high starting point for salary negotiations should he be successful in his search for a new role. The rationale is that he is not harming anyone, simply looking out for himself.

- A respected banker is given more change at the supermarket counter than she should receive – she has more than enough time to go back and return the excess money, but gets in her car and drives off – feeling "lucky". The rationalisation is that she did not influence the supermarket salesperson to make the mistake in the first place.

These are only a few examples of the world we live in today. You may have heard of, or have been involved in similar activities in the past. As an Emerging Leader, you will have to discipline yourself to be honourable, truthful and faithful in the little things. This is how you build up your "integrity muscles" and as such prepare yourself for the time you will have to make a difficult call affecting many lives.

As I conclude this section, I will paraphrase for all Emerging Leaders the advice that my father, Justus Oluyomi Odukoya gave me as a young man. *"It takes years to define your values, set moral standards to live by, build a reputation for integrity and develop the character to sustain that reputation... it however takes one minute of an indiscretion or a slight lowering of the standards you set for yourself to lose it all. Once you have lost the integrity platform, you lose the respect, honour and trust that came with it. And when you lose them, it is at least twice as difficult to reclaim them. Whatever ground you gained by allowing yourself to slip below your standards will be nothing compared to the shame of your fall and the difficulty of climbing back to the top"*

Examine - Equip - Emerge

Authenticity and Integrity

1. Leaders will always be weighed upon by great expectations from their stakeholders. How do you manage the ongoing pressure of expectations in your journey as a leader?

....

....

....

....

....

2. How have you been able to turn the pressure of expectation into a force to galvanise you for successful delivery?

....

....

....

....

....

3. What is self-awareness and what is its importance to your authenticity as an Emerging Leader?

....

....

....

....

....

4. You are not born as an authentic leader. Your authenticity is developed over time from what you have become through life and learning. Can you look into your past and list 5 key points of history, learning or experience that has shaped the leader you are today?

    ....
    ....
    ....
    ....
    ....

5. The author gives an example of "respect" as a core value that forms part of his identity. What are the top 3 core values that you hold as key to who you are?

    ....
    ....
    ....
    ....
    ....

6. What are the dangers to a leader who operates as a "photocopy" of her leaders rather than a true depiction of herself?

    ....
    ....
    ....
    ....
    ....

7. This chapter features a story of integrity displayed by a Human Resources Manager. What does integrity mean to you and how important do you think it is to you as an Emerging Leader?

    ....
    ....
    ....
    ....
    ....

8. Which people – family, friends, colleagues or even those you never met personally – have you learnt the most from as you have moved through your life journey?

    ....
    ....
    ....
    ....

9. What are the top 3 lessons you have learnt from yourself that have changed the way you view life?

    ....
    ....
    ....
    ....
    ....

10. What values do you hold especially precious that you would not violate?

    Are these values "inherited" from people you look up to?

    Are these values "realized" from within your self-awareness?

How impactful have these values been on your life?

....

....

....

....

11. Can you list three key attributes that people have seen in you, and would vouch for concerning you – regardless of external stimuli?

....

....

....

12. How have you handled challenges to your integrity [the temptation to temporarily ditch the real you] in the past? How would you handle such challenges going forward?

....

....

....

....

....

13. How close to being an authentic leader are you? What do you need to do in order to "get there"?

....

....

....

....

....

14. Which of your currently held values and standards will be
   most difficult to defend in the face of temptation? Do you have
   a plan to ensure that you do not fall?

   ....

   ....

   ....

   ....

   ....

*"One of the truest tests of integrity is its blunt refusal to be
compromised".*
– Chinua Achebe

Energizing Excellence

"Excellence is not a skill; it is an attitude.
– Ralph Marston

One of the key responsibilities and expectations of leaders is the injection of positive energy into people, processes and projects that they are involved with or have responsibility for. This injection of positive energy is what is translated by many as "influence" – the evidence of leadership. It is often said that a failing organisation is the product of a tired leadership – one who has switched from energizing to an energy-sapping mode. This is how important leadership is.

> It is often said that a failing organisation is the product of a tired leadership – one who has switched from energizing to an energy-sapping mode. This is how important leadership is.

WHAT KIND OF LEADER ARE YOU?
Leadership studies have shown over the years that there are a variety of ways through which a leader can exert positive influence within an organisation or community.

THE MESSAGE LEADERS
Some leaders exert influence through their great oratory skills.

They are such good communicators. They know when to speak, and when not to speak. They know which words to use and those to avoid. They are acutely aware of people's cultures and background and they factor this into their communication. They have full control over the tone, diction, flow and content of their communication. Body language and emotional state management forms a part of their communicative genius. The great Dr. Martin Luther King, well known for his iconic speech *"I have a dream"* would easily fall into this category, just like the former Prime Minister of Great Britain, *Tony Blair* and the previous Chelsea Football Club Manager, *Jose Mourinho*, would. These individuals are able to make people believe in a better destination or sell a vision so well that there is a positive change in the attitudes of those who they communicate with. I call these kinds of leaders the *"Message Leaders"*.

The message leader speaks with such authority that it is almost impossible to fault his message. The listener is captivated either instantly or over a period of time, and the message becomes the reason for following the leader. The message leader also delivers the message with such belief that resonates with the target audience and creates "faith by association" in the destination being presented. Even when such leaders are known [and sceptically viewed] for their "way with words," they get through to some of the more distrusting members of their target audience. In other words, they are able to communicate effectively, and therefore influence or lead others. As an Emerging Leader, "messaging" is one key leadership skill that can unlock doors and can make your leadership journey smoother than it can be.

EXEMPLARY LEADERS

Other leaders exert considerable influence through the power of endeavour. Perhaps, you have come across leaders of this ilk, or are you one? I call this group the *"Exemplary Leaders"*. These leaders shine through their tireless and industrious approach to work; they believe in the purpose of the work as well as the benefits that accrue from it. Many of such leaders get to the office before anyone else, and are usually the last to leave. Others may not spend such long hours at work, but in the short time spent, they go through such tremendous amounts of work, delivering top value at an incredible pace that you wonder what they have in their cereal every morning. Even when conventional timings say that "work time" is over, their minds are at work.

Years ago, I worked with GE and the legend Jeff Immelt. This CEO was well known; his work ethic was exceptional. He reportedly worked 100 hours per week for more than 20 years, a stretch that earned him the nickname *"The Bionic Manager"* in some quarters. *Indra Nooyi*, the Pepsi CEO is said to have worked the graveyard shift – midnight to 5am as a receptionist in order to pay her way through her Master's degree at Yale. As CEO, she regularly worked up to 60 hours a week, challenging her team to walk the walk with her.

In my experience working with various multinational organisations, these Exemplary Leaders have been important to the building of morale by "associative mentorship". This is when colleagues at various levels are energised by connecting with the working persona of the leader. The fact that one leader can achieve so much through hard work serves as a reference point for workers who need the proverbial 'kick up the rear end.' Even those workers already doing well are able to appreciate leaders who lead by example.

RELATIONAL LEADERS

There are yet other leaders who are well known for influencing others through their relational, interpersonal and people-motivating skills. This class of leaders effortlessly create a desire to give 100% and more to the joint cause. There is an aura exuded by these leaders that sends out the *"it's good to be here at work"* message. It is more than just how or what they communicate, more than the competence they show at work. They affect people and it can be difficult to pin down how they are so effective in doing that. Moreover, if you were to ask people in the workplace what traits in their leaders they find motivating, there would be a mix of expected traits including: *trustworthiness, respect, inclusiveness, competence, expertise,* and *exemplary behaviour.* Perhaps a good example of a "motivator-leader" is **Harry Redknapp** – an experienced British football manager known for his time with West Ham United, Portsmouth and Tottenham Hotspur football clubs. When speaking in 2015, Rafael Van der Vaart [a former Tottenham Hotspur football player] said of Mr. Redknapp, *"And Harry — he was like your dad. I would give everything for that man; I was really sad when he left."* .Another

> **For all three influence styles discussed above [message-leader, exemplar-leader and motivator-leader], the impact they are able to exert depends to a great extent on their *attitude* towards the people they work with and their *passion* for the work they do.**

prominent example is **Magatte Wade**, an African entrepreneur who has started and successfully led two African themed organisations [*Adina World Beverage* and *Tiossan*]. Ms. Wade has since been featured on the BBC, CNN, FOX Business news channels and serves as a mentor for the MIT Legatum Centre for Entrepreneurship and Development.

> **It remains the responsibility of any individual to understand the principles of excellence and become determined to apply them to various aspects of life.**

It is pertinent to note that these avenues of influence are not the exclusive playgrounds of persons who run teams, departments, organisations or governments. All these forms of influence can be – and are frequently exerted by workers on the so-called "shop floor", interns, new supervisors just as well as a CEO can. I have been part of many teams and working groups where persons with no formal or positional leadership titles have been the driving force behind the success of projects and the team as a whole.

ABILITY, ATTITUDE AND PASSION

As an Emerging Leader, you already have various pre-built abilities – sometimes hidden and untrained, but present, nevertheless. Your time in school, college, university or in work experience serves to "educate" these abilities, preparing them for the times and situations that will require their use. However, what separates the forefront leaders from the rest is the attitude with which the education is approached and the passion with which these abilities or gifts are applied. Indeed, attitude and passion are two key foundation stones of excellence. For all three influence styles discussed above [message-leader, exemplar-leader and motivator-leader], the impact they are able to exert depends to a great extent on their *attitude* towards the people they work with and their *passion* for the work they do.

> "no matter how much knowledge or wealth you acquire, there will always be room for improvement."

Indeed, the potent combination of ability, attitude and passion will separate the great leaders from the pretenders every time. This combination is the recipe for excellence. I have come to understand that it is not just what you do as a leader that defines you as an excellent leader – the how and why you do what you do it is rather more important. The "how" speaks to the attitude and the "why" informs the passion with which you do things.

A very personal example of this is my father. I watched him lead his family through good times, bad times and indifferent times with the same attitude. He had a positive, relentless and giving nature that kept him going all seasons. Like every man, he had his flaws, but I saw a lot of good in the way he protected and loved his family – and I find that a lot of the values I hold today come from what I witnessed as a child and as a growing man. He had that drive for excellence – even in the small details [he could iron a shirt better than most

> However, as an Emerging Leader, you must have an inner conviction of your purpose and value.

laundry professionals] that placed him above many of his contemporaries.

NATURE OF EXCELLENCE

Having defined the combination of ability, attitude and passion as the recipe for excellence, it becomes important for me to provide additional information on the nature of excellence as well as tips to help Emerging Leaders attain and maintain a lifestyle that encourages and delivers excellence as standard. The following statements will help in that direction:

Anyone can attain and maintain excellence; however, there is no guarantee that everyone will do so. Indeed, our world today shows enough evidence that whilst the principles guiding leadership excellence are well known, there will always be people who will not or cannot follow these principles. As I have mentioned elsewhere in this book and in my leadership training sessions, nobody can force leadership excellence on anyone. It remains the responsibility of any individual to understand the principles of excellence and become determined to apply them to various aspects of life. For every person who commits to excellence, there will probably be at least, one other who cannot be bothered to do so, or who will not be placed in an environment that encourages excellence. As a team leader and manager, I have been privileged to review the performance of team members. This opened my eyes to the wide variance in attitude and passion [between people with similar levels of ability]. **My submission is that attitude and passion make ability more effective and as a result, more impactful.**

Excellence is not a defined point or destination – it is a continuous commitment to a journey of improvement. This is an important attribute of excellence that all Emerging Leaders must understand and embrace in order to deliver the expected value in their assignment. Excellence is continuously innovating, continuously creating and never arriving at a "terminal". As an Emerging Leader, you must see your call to leadership as a continuum of assessment, improvement and application. The honest and critical *assessment* of the impact you currently have on your organisation is combined almost seamlessly with your on-going efforts at *improving* yourself, as well as *applying* the "improved you" to various leadership situations and questions. Many stories have been told of how some of the best sportsmen, entertainers and entrepreneurs are simply those who invest the most time and effort into continuous improvement. These persons appreciate each new milestone but never get sucked into the "feeling of arrival". Each milestone is celebrated with good measure, and seen as the stepping stone for the next set of milestones. As I mentioned earlier, my father was a great influence in my life. One of his pearls of wisdom was "no matter how much knowledge or wealth you acquire, there will always be room for improvement." I never forgot this. And today, as a father myself, I find myself happily walking the path of continuous improvement and teaching the same principle to my children.

The delivery of excellence elevates you into situations where you operate at levels higher than you are used to. Each time you hit a level of service that is considered excellent; the reward is usually an expectation of higher service levels. We never expect less than what was previously delivered. This is a principle built into the very essence of life. With each passing day, we grow in physical dimensions – and in some ways that are not readily visible. **Growth, like excellence, is not a status, rather, a concept that supports the very real potential that tomorrow can be better than today.** Some of the team leaders I have had as a young software engineer were quite good at keeping me looking for the next level. With each good service delivery, I was given a dose of thanks, followed swiftly by a challenge that stretched my ability and extended my horizons. These challenges were within reach enough to be considered "doable" but also out of reach enough to make me call on abilities I did not know I had in me. The key in all of this development was that it was I - the "growing person" who had to size up the next target, summon up belief and relish the challenge of reaching the next level. This "next level" process is now ingrained into my consciousness and forms part of the leader I have become today.

Excellence is not being satisfied with equalling or beating the achievements of others, it is the noble and on-going challenge of seeking out the targets no one else even saw. This is something I consistently teach my children and have included in training sessions for leaders and managers over the years. It is important that Emerging Leaders do not define themselves by what others have or have not done. I am not advocating that you ignore the achievements of other leaders or the advice of your mentors – indeed, these must be fully appreciated. However, as an Emerging Leader, you must have an inner conviction of your purpose and value. This inner conviction is what will generate the passion in you to succeed even in the face of opposition, challenge and unfavourable conditions. This inner conviction is what will drive your transformation into the best possible Emerging Leader you can be. This "best of you" is the one that derives great satisfaction and challenge in delivering high quality value to your team, organisation or community. This is the "you" who leaves an indelible and unmistakable mark of quality on every person who comes into contact with you, every task you complete and every situation you manage. This is the "you" who – much like the early morning sun, affects the day – provides light and energy to your environment. I submit that this is the "you" that you are looking for – and the one your world is waiting for!

I leave you with a few questions that will help you apply the contents of this chapter practically.

Examine - Equip - Emerge

Energizing Excellence

1. What does the concept of influence mean to you? Please give an example of when you have been a good influence on others or have had others influence you positively.

   ....
   ....
   ....
   ....
   ....

2. The author shows three types of influencers... Which of these categories would you say comes more naturally to you? Do you see yourself as strong in more than one?

   ....
   ....
   ....
   ....
   ....

3. What does the author describe as the three ingredients that form the recipe for excellence? How much of each ingredient have you seen in yourself? Can you improve on these?

   ....
   ....
   ....
   ....

4. Anyone can attain and maintain excellence; however, there is no guarantee that everyone will do so. What does this mean to you?

   ....
   ....
   ....
   ....
   ....

5. Excellence is not a defined point or destination – it is a continuous commitment to a journey of improvement. How does this assertion affect your quest for improvement as a leader?

   ....
   ....
   ....
   ....
   ....

6. The delivery of excellence elevates you into situations where you operate at levels higher than you are used to. What levels are you aiming for and how do you plan to get there?

   ....
   ....
   ....
   ....
   ....

7. Excellence is not being satisfied with equalling or beating the

achievements of others – it is the noble and ongoing challenge of seeking out the targets no one else even saw. How excited are you by the pursuits you are currently working on and how daring is your dream?

....

....

....

....

....

8. Can you identify what it is about your mentor or manager that "energizes" you?

....

....

....

....

....

9. Can you identify what it is about yourself that "energizes" you?

....

....

....

....

....

10. What would you say is your most effective skill? How can you make yourself even better at what you do best?

....

....
....
....
....

11. What plans do you have to release your knowledge to others so as to improve or energize them?

....
....
....
....
....

12. Can you re-live your best feeling of satisfaction that came from using your energizing excellence to improve others?

....
....
....
....

"Excellence is the result of caring more than others think is wise, risking more than others think is safe, dreaming more than others think is practical, and expecting more than others think is possible."
- Ronnie Oldham

chapter 5

Champions Courage

"And David said to Solomon his son, be strong and of good courage, and do it..."
— 1st Chronicles 28:20

There is something incredibly infectious about the spirit, person, achievements and drive of a champion. As many will attest, this effect leaves a mark on those who observe the champion do his or her "thing". Whether you want to or not, you feel an affinity towards the champion – and you go through various levels of anxiety, expectation, fear, confidence, belief, despair and even elation depending on what the champion is going through during a game or event. It really does not matter whether the champion [or in some cases, team] is aware of your existence – you just want to be part of the success story.

In the United Kingdom, where football [soccer to my American friends] is almost a religion, there are some Monday mornings [after the Saturday and Sunday games] that draw a line between friends; some arrive at work carrying what are known as "bragging rights" – and others would rather take the day off after watching their team suffer a humbling defeat at the hands of the local rivals. I support a football club known as Tottenham Hotspur, and I have been on both sides of this emotional fence many times.

Through the years, I have watched and nailed my support to the flags of quite a few champions of the sporting, political and business worlds. The likes of Muhammad Ali [Boxing], Pelé [football], Bill Gates [technology and business] and Nelson Mandela [human rights and politics] ignited something inside of me that made me sit up and take notice of what they did, how they did it and the results they achieved. This interest in many instances developed into a desire to know how they did what they did – and eventually into a self-drive to learn how to apply their methods and principles to my life. Needless to say, I have never met any of these people. There are also quite a few other inspirational persons who I have learnt from, from afar but never had the opportunity to sit with and discuss.

> **These people had their moments of brilliance, as well as their very human moments of failing. They were as much exponents of excellence as they were examples of human fallibility.**

When I reflect on the impact that these champions and leaders have had on me, I am also able to see that these people had their moments of brilliance, as well as their very human moments of failing. They were as much exponents of excellence as they were examples of human fallibility. However, their flaws are somehow dwarfed out by their excellence in the areas of strength. People still see them as champions and identify with the good and beautiful stuff they've produced.

> **I believe that the intrinsic driving forces behind the decision are rather more important than the decision itself**

THE CHAMPION SPIRIT

As a teacher in Leadership, I have spent time trying to identify which trait in these champions mostly impacted me. Over the last 2 years, I have conducted informal research – asking more than 100 different persons what they found as the most inspiring or most impacting trait of their heroes. The simple answer, although given in a variety of ways is that while the results and achievements are important tools of motivation, the "spirit of the champion" is the singularly most impactful trait. This is that invisible but common "thing" that transforms a laid-back easy going young man into a tiger on the rugby park, or a caring and friendly mother into a ruthless negotiator in the boardroom. This spirit is responsible for the additional 10% that champions purportedly give, above the usual 100%. This audacious spirit enables entrepreneurs to take that one extra step on the risk scale – re-mortgaging their twice-mortgaged house to fund an idea. This same drive propels a boxer to come out for three more minutes of "facial re-arrangement" in the pursuit of a World Title. This is what I call the Champion's Courage.

As an Emerging Leader, courage is a must-have item in your leadership tool-box. It is one of the key differences between those who "do" and those who "promise to do." Wayne Gretzky, the Canadian ice hockey player famously said that "you miss 100% of the shots you do not take" – a clear pointer to the importance of being daring enough to do what needs to be done. It is commonly said that leaders live or die by their decisions. While I agree with this statement in principle, I believe that the **intrinsic driving forces** behind the decision are rather more important than the decision itself. Courage is one such driving force from within the leader's mind. The level of courage and conviction that informs a leader's decision will determine the effectiveness of that decision – and by extension, of the actions taken in implementing that decision.

> If you want to emerge as a leader despite the challenges that stand in your way, you must have the courage of a champion – the kind of courage that accepts the fight ahead and goes all out to compete fairly for the few available opportunities.

Like many parents [and some of you would have experienced this], I enrolled my children for swimming lessons at a very young age. Once we got past the stage where I had to take the child into the pool, I would sit in the stands and watch the teachers put them through the various learning stages. I remember when one of my sons would simply refuse to jump into the pool with his mates. He was okay using the steps to lower himself into the pool – jumping in was however a different thing altogether. His decision not to jump was driven by a lack of courage [not the same as fear]. He was not afraid of the water; he was simply not courageous enough to jump in! Many months later, without being prompted or cajoled by anyone, he jumped in with his mates. When I congratulated him on his progress, I also asked him what changed. He said, "I simply decided that it was okay to jump in this time." In other words, he simply gave himself permission to jump in. This is exactly how courage affects leaders, and why leaders need courage in order to be effective.

> Quit waiting for things to come easy, but rather, prepare your mind to put your best into seeking and achieving the goals you have set for yourself.

The rest of this chapter explores the different aspects of an Emerging Leader's life that can be made better or worse, based on the level of courage demonstrated by the leader. Quite a few illustrations from past and present leaders reveal the impact that courage can and does have on leadership.

COURAGE: THINKING BIG.

The mind of the Emerging Leader is the birthplace of the ideas that this and future generations are looking for. Every invention that shaped our world started out as ideas in the mind of somebody, somewhere. These ideas – that would have seemed overly ambitious when they were first proposed have now become the mainstay of some of our greatest achievements in science, technology and other areas of the economy. For instance, it would be difficult to imagine where our civilisation would be without a certain Alexander Graham Bell and his telephone or without the courage displayed by the Wright Brothers and their ground-breaking plane flight. Thinking big is a product of courage. As an Emerging Leader, you will find yourself continually in the place where answers to questions yet to be clarified are required. At times, you will be expected to set strategies for existing ideas that everyone knows are "completely impossible to implement". This is where courage – and indeed champion-level courage will be your best tool. This is where you dare to dream of the impossible and back your dream to be realised.

COURAGE: SEIZING OPPORTUNITIES.

We live in a world where success and failure are separated by very fine lines. For leaders looking to emerge in a chosen career path [say, Project Management], they look around and find the challenge set by other competitive project managers with similar academic records, similar experience to fall back on and similar determination to succeed. Effectively, the continuously increasing supply of willing and able leaders, combined with the reduced demand for service has made opportunities difficult to come by. The competition in the job market is fierce – and the same applies in the entrepreneurs' battleground. The effect of this market competition is exacerbated by various global and regional economic factors. If you want to emerge as a leader despite the challenges that stand in your way, you must have the courage of a champion – the kind of courage that accepts the fight ahead and goes all out to compete fairly for the few available opportunities. The truth is, you will win some of the battles and lose some – however, the key is never to fear the fight. So, the next time you bid for a contract as one of 100 potential winners, don't hold back on your bid. The next time you go for a promotion amongst an array of eminently qualified colleagues, make sure you compete with all you have. Quit waiting for things to come easy, but rather, prepare your mind to put your best into seeking and achieving the goals you have set for yourself. While your courage is not a golden guarantee for success, it most certainly has the power to boost your confidence when you get what you set out to achieve, and keep you going for the times when things work out

> **The Emerging Leader is therefore not exempt from the "ups and downs" of life's rollercoaster. Indeed, as a leader, you are expected to be quite adept at managing yourself through various situations while also providing leadership for others.**

the way you do not expect. Prior to joining Citigroup, I was told by a recruitment agent that my lack of banking experience [I had never even worked next door to a bank] would hamper my chances. This agent refused to submit my application on that basis. Undeterred, I sought out a rival agency that was prepared to match my courage with his. It turned out that the challenge posed to me only served to fuel my fighting spirit. I eventually got the job and that kick-started my career in the banking sector. Now, as I spend time developing leaders within the industry, I encourage them to approach challenges with the courage of a champion.

COURAGE: DEALING WITH AND MANAGING CHANGE.

If there is anything that could make or break an Emerging Leader, it is quite likely to be how change is perceived, managed or led. Leadership, by definition, is all about change. Change can be initiated by a leader or prompted by external forces or parties. Change may be organisational, economic, political, community-related, legal, cultural, professional, operational, policy-related or be rooted in a wide range of personal situations [e.g. marital, health, family, financial, career...].

In my experience of leading and training leaders, I have seen leadership effectiveness hinged on the way a leader handles change. Whatever the nature of the change and however it is initiated, it is of vital importance that Emerging Leaders have the right attitude towards change. The key to finding the right answers to questions posed by change is for Emerging Leaders to have the courage to let go of the familiar. In doing this, the leader also loses the fear of the new and can expect to enjoy the challenges ahead.

During my career with global banking organisations, I have been privileged to take up a key role within Information Technology that had been held by the same individual for nearly a decade. My predecessor was seen as highly capable and extremely effective. In my handover dealings with him, I also found him to be quite personable, knowledgeable and professional. The speech he gave at his leave-taking would not have been out of place at a valedictory service for an outgoing president. Three weeks into my tenure, I started noting processes and procedures that he had put in place that I knew needed upgrading or changing. As a leader, I had to deal with my predecessor's almost god-like status, a dwindling budget allocation and an aggressive "resource relocation" strategy in proposing my changes. I needed the conviction that a leader's courage gives to propose, initiate and follow through with the changes. Some of that courage was rooted in my professional experience but the bulk of a champion's courage comes from his character. **Courage is the expression of who you really are in the time of change and conflict – it is the expression of your character.**

Many years ago, whilst working with one of the largest banking groups in the world, I found myself as a team leader, in the unenviable position of having to select 6 out of 12 members of my team for "role redundancy notification." Those reading this can attest to the fact that this can be difficult – especially in a closely-knit team environment. As team leader, I also had to sit in with the Human Resources Manager and personally deliver the bad news.

Following on from this, I had to manage the same team [including the individuals who were losing their jobs] for a period of 3 months according to the organisation's policy. During these months, I had to deal with flagging team morale, troughs in team effectiveness, varying emotional states of the team members [not only those who were leaving]; senior management expectations for knowledge transfer, and offshore vendors, as well as my personal state of mind – all rising from a change that I did not initiate [and would not have chosen to initiate]. It did take courage to be the leader that my team really needed during that period - courage to be manager, leader, friend, counsellor and support mechanism.

COURAGE: PRESSING ON IN DIFFICULT TIMES.
Life can be a mixed bag of celebrations and commiserations, an unpredictable, yet exciting ride through the time continuum. Most people can look back and recount times of great success as well as periods that were decidedly not as enjoyable. The Emerging Leader is therefore not exempt from the "ups and downs" of life's rollercoaster. Indeed, as a leader, you are expected to be quite adept at managing yourself through various situations while also providing leadership for others. In the business context, leaders are the go-to persons when the constants suddenly become variables and the unexpected becomes the current reality.

I stood by the window in an adjoining office building one desperately difficult afternoon, watching fellow professionals stream out of the then Lehman Brothers building on Bank Street, E14 – following the collapse of their organisation. Over the next week, as the full scale of the carnage caused by the financial crisis unfolded, I spoke with a close friend who worked with another organisation that had collapsed during the crisis. He described the days preceding and following the collapse of his organisation as the darkest hours of his professional life. The feeling of uncertainty and helplessness mixed with disdain with which bankers were viewed, made that period a sore test for the most patient of us. Although my friend did find a way out of the situation, many were not as fortunate or blessed as he was. As a result, many cases of depression, divorce, destitution and even death have been traced directly or indirectly to the financial crisis.

As an Emerging Leader, you will learn more about your leadership credentials and qualities in difficult times than you will in the fair seasons of life. All leaders must expect tests and challenging times and must display courage to keep them going when things don't look bright. Leaders like Martin Luther King, who emerged in times when even his skin colour marked him for disadvantage, were effectively built up by their relentless drive to see their goals achieved. In the face of pressure from various adversaries, Dr. King showed remarkable courage to convey his message to his intended audience. Even though for many years, nothing looked like it was changing, he pressed on.

The biblical story of Joseph describes a young man's journey through exceptional difficulty, including strained relationships at home with his brothers. As the story unfolds, we see a young man rise to prominent leadership through the strength of character built in adversity. The courage to keep going when the freeborn Joseph became a slave and then a prisoner, is what made the difference. In order to emerge into your place of influence, you need courage like this young man- Joseph.

COURAGE: SEEKING HELP IN TIMES OF NEED.
It is quite common for people to view leaders as almost "super-human," especially when the leader has a good track record of success or has been particularly impactful in the community, workplace or the home. Young leaders are especially susceptible to what I call the "superman syndrome." This is because they are naturally energetic and usually approach life and leadership with the confidence and arrogance expected of youth.

As a youth leader and coach over the last 20 years, I have had the privilege of working with quite a few amazing young leaders in churches across London and the Midlands in the UK. The young leader is typically an exciting mix of optimism, confidence [bordering on the arrogant], disregard [for constituted authority], raw ability and resilience. These characteristics can turn the young leader [especially those who rise to the top quickly] into the focus of hero-worship where people label them as the next "big thing." Hero worship of this nature can also lead to young leaders believing in their own apparent invincibility.

I recently read the story of a young woman whose father is a well-known musician. The veteran musician told the story of how his daughter grew up and mingled with a group of friends where certain drugs and alcohol were consumed in quantities and at frequencies that surpassed the norm. As expected, the daring and confidence of youth led the young woman to chart her own life path independent of parental control. After seeing two of her friends die from drug and alcohol related issues – she picked up the phone and said these four words *"Dad, I need help."* It takes courage to know when your strength, knowledge or ability can no longer get you through difficult situations. Irrespective of previous achievements and on-going success, it is important for Emerging Leaders to identify the support mechanism required for the tough times – and to use such support wisely.

Answering the questions at the end of this chapter will help you recognise your current level of courage and show you how you can exercise courage in various situations.

Examine – Equip - Emerge

Champions Courage - Chapter 5

1. When things get difficult or challenging, what do you do? Do you find solace and strength by retreating into yourself with the aim of coming back in style or do you consciously square up to the issue and look to resolve it?

   ....
   ....
   ....
   ....
   ....

2. How do you convince yourself to press on with an idea or a project, especially when there are people who openly oppose your position?

   ....
   ....
   ....
   ....
   ....

3. What are your greatest fears as a leader?

   ....
   ....
   ....
   ....

4. Which of your fears [or phobias] have you successfully faced and defeated?

    ....
    ....
    ....
    ....
    ....

5. How much better do you get when you deal with difficult situations?

    ....
    ....
    ....
    ....
    ....

6. Are you the type of character who will publicly take a stand against an oppressive leader or one who prefers to deliver value by supporting another person's stand?

    ....
    ....
    ....
    ....
    ....

7. Who are the champions [in any walk of life] that have been most inspirational to you – and how have they helped shape who you are as a leader today?

    ....

....

....

....

....

8. Thinking big is a by-product of courage. What are the big ideas that you have considered and how driven are you to bring them from conception to manifestation?

....

....

....

....

....

9. A Champion's Courage is about seizing opportunities, even when nothing seems to be possible. How would you prepare your mind to keep going for the top prize in times of challenges?

....

....

....

....

....

10. In life, change happens but it is not always welcome. It may not also be favourable to the leader. What is your attitude to unwanted change – and how has this attitude helped you in your leadership journey?

....

....

....

....

....

Courage is contagious. When a brave man takes a stand, the spines of others are often stiffened.
-   Billy Graham

chapter 6

3 D's Desire, Dedication, Discipline

*If you set goals and go after them
with all the determination you can muster,
your gifts will take you places that will amaze you.*
-Les Brown

The story of any leader is usually told from the achievement viewpoint – with focus on the impact of such achievements as well as how such achievements were arrived at. As an Emerging Leader, your success will be measured as a direct function of what you are able to deliver. **Effectively, whatever you can envision in your mind and bring to life will be your legacy to your world.** I have understood this ever since I learnt to sing that popular hymn with the words *"only remembered by what we have done."*

Every achievement starts in the mind of the leader as an idea. The most powerful product of the human mind is the idea. Ideas are the precursor of all human effort. My experience as a leader and a leadership development practitioner has taught me that an idea does not become an achievement off its steam. **The Emerging Leader must possess certain attributes and have a mindset that drives the implementation of the idea.** This chapter examines three key characteristics that must form a part of the Emerging Leader's toolkit – Desire, Determination and Discipline.

THE POWER OF DESIRE

Desire is a powerful force of the human mind – a force that is manifested as a deep longing for a specific outcome. It is considered the foundation of all human actions. Philosophers and scholars, in spite of their many disagreements on the subject of *desire*, agree that it can be as strong a force for the negative as it can be for the positive. Desire is a force, which if left unchecked can take control of a person's outlook on life and trigger actions that are out of character for that individual. Emerging Leaders, like everyone else, have desires and are subject to the ebb and flow of emotion that these desires can bring.

> **Leadership can be a lonely, cruel and demanding place – therefore it is not enough to want to lead. As an Emerging Leader, it is important that you have a strong desire to lead rooted in a deep conviction of your purpose.**

> **Every leader must be encouraged by the strength of their desire to be the solution – desire to think differently from the crowd, desire to walk the paths that others are afraid of and the desire to lead.**

Leadership can be a lonely, cruel and demanding place – therefore it is not enough to **want** to lead. As an Emerging Leader, it is important that you have a strong **desire** to lead. This desire must be rooted in a deep conviction of your purpose. As you grow through life, you will have numerous conversations with yourself about being a leader in the sector that you know you have the talent to influence.

Emerging everyday into the family, community or marketplace requires a force that is potent enough to lift the leader above the conflicts, confusions and challenges that will come. Parents must lead their families through the uncertainties that their world presents. Community leaders must uphold the law, defend the interests of the people and be humane – all at once. Leaders in the workplace must be on top of finance, policy, process, people, performance and then some more. The place of leadership is the place of high stakes and high expectations. Every leader must be encouraged by the strength of their desire to be the solution – desire to think differently from the crowd, desire to walk the paths that others are afraid of and the desire to lead.

When you study leaders who are either at the top of their profession or have had major impact on their world, you will see men and women whose desire to lead was stronger than the reasons to hide. These are people whose desire to lead enabled them to challenge the status-quo in different areas. Their desire to lead moved them to the front of the pack because they dared to have dreams that were based on their desires. Even though their desire could have come across as pure madness, especially to those who did not have the same vision, they stayed on course. You will need this force of desire to emerge into your leadership assignment day after day, year after year. Although I agree that desire in itself will not make anyone a great leader, it is still a very potent tool any leader needs to maintain his conviction and keep the fire of passion burning.

I was told the story of a young woman who arrived in Europe from a war-torn North African state. This young woman had lived through the bitterness of war, rape, terror and the attendant hopelessness of the refugee camps. Barely able to read and write, she set about making a new life for herself in the United Kingdom. Eight years later, after her adult education [during which she also joined two women empowerment community groups and set up a mentoring scheme for young disadvantaged girls], this amazing woman graduated from university with honours and is currently building a career at a major international organisation]. When asked about the secret of her successful life turnaround, she simply said *"I had a desire in my heart to succeed, and my desire refused to be silenced by the challenges I faced."*

I have met many Emerging Leaders who are blessed with an array of talents and abilities – a combination of natural attributes and a desire for continuous improvement. Such multi-talented leaders, quite often, are confronted with multiple expectations from friends, family, colleagues and clients, which in turn fires up additional pressure from within the leader. If you are such a leader, you will need to fall back on the desire in you – that will burn stronger for some outcomes than for others. Understanding desire will help you harness your abilities and prioritise your actions. This understanding of desire will help to clarify purpose and set life goals. It will also protect you from the pressure of guilt that can arise when choices are made to pursue one course of action over the other. Understanding and harnessing desire makes you a more effective leader with greater confidence in your decision-making.

As an Emerging Leader, you would need to ask yourself the following questions:

- How strong is my desire to lead?
- What do I desire most to achieve as a leader?
- What issue or problem do I desire most to solve as a leader?
- What am I willing to let go of in order to serve my leadership ability?

> **Your determination must be borne out of a belief in the vision you have for a future that improves or builds up.**

UNCOMMON DETERMINATION

Determination is the positive and motivational state of mind that works with the desire in a leader to drive the conversion of ideas into activity and by extension, activity into desired result. Determination is the resoluteness and firmness of purpose that all Emerging Leaders must apply in order to leave a desired impact in whatever assignment or situation they face. Determination is often the difference maker between the "nearly there" and the "really there" leaders. Effectively, determination is a crucially important link between desire and destination.

As a leadership consultant, I have observed and interviewed a wide spectrum of leaders – from the "new kids on the block" to the "wise elder statesmen," examining amongst other things, how much more effective and impactful they are through determination. One leader – an Executive Director in the trading division of a well-known London-based investment bank said to me, "*determination is what convinces me that an empty fuel tank is not the end of my journey.*" The sentiments of a community leader

I met in West Africa were along the same lines - *"determination is the fire in my belly that keeps me coming back for more when things appear not to be working."* An impressive young leader I worked with briefly in Pune, India said to me that *"determination is the anticipation of celebration – and therefore the reason I smile in every situation."* While they all use different words to define the same term, these viewpoints show that determination is clearly a valuable part of a leader's make-up.

As an Emerging Leader, it is certain that you will face periods of difficulty, uncertainty or challenge that will require you to draw on something extra from within you. It is widely believed that how a leader comes out of challenging situations is an indication of that leader's likelihood to be successful in navigating through future challenges. Whether you are a beleaguered political leader fighting to stabilise the economy of a country, a parent having to support a child through difficult stages of life or a business owner trying to drive through enough sales to survive, the principle remains true that *"tough situations build character, and character is the stability of leadership."* I have extracted four constituent elements of determination that you must experience as an Emerging Leader if you are to be the solution to the issues in your world that you are meant to – and can – be.

DETERMINATION TO SEE A DIFFERENT OR BETTER OUTCOME. Leadership, as I have alluded to earlier, is result-based. Leaders, by definition, are committed to an on-going drive from the known to the desired reality. Strategies, objectives and goals are what leaders breathe and live by. The greatest leaders are those with an unshakeable belief in the better outcome or the different reality that is on a higher level than the current reality. This unshakeable belief is manifested in the steely, uncompromising attitude known as *determination*.

The clarity and strength of your perception of the destination will inspire the people who will believe in your vision and who will run the difficult terrain that leads to vision fulfilment with you. The former President of the Republic of South Africa, Dr. Nelson Mandela was able to motivate and encourage people who were in need of a solution to their problems. He did not only speak of his vision for a new and fairer South Africa, he demonstrated an uncompromising determination to see the manifestation of that vision. His determination in turn fuelled a global movement that helped bring an end to the minority rule in South Africa and launched a new political order in the country.

> In recent years in the English Premier League, footballers such as Steven Gerrard, Rio Ferdinand and David Beckham have been celebrated – not just for their talent, but for the discipline and application they consistently exhibited through many years of playing the game at the highest level

It is important to sound a note of caution here to all leaders. You must be able to differentiate between stubborn foolhardiness and determination. Your determination must be borne out of a belief in the vision you have for a future that improves or builds up. Many leaders have failed because they had a wrong mentality that doggedly going down one path [irrespective of its merits or demerits] is a hallmark of good leadership. My observation of leadership concepts and practicalities has shown me that the people who follow leaders [being leaders in their own rights] are quite adept at assessing the leader's character and making informed judgments on the effectiveness of any leader.

Determination to succeed is usually admirable in leaders – because it can set the tone for others within a team, organisation or community to follow. When those around you see you approach difficult situations with determination and they can see that your determination is driven by clarity of purpose, as well as conviction in doing the right thing, they feed off your leadership and possess deeper understanding of what you are doing. This is when you have the team, organisation or community pulling together in support of a leader. They find a belief in what you believe, they find strength in your determination, and become strong enough to back you when you are struggling; they stand with you – ready to fall with you if required. As you continually emerge into your place of leadership – be it your job, your family or your community, you really want your level of determination to pull such reactions out from those around you! This is when the challenging road of leadership is made a little more rewarding.

> **Ultimately, a leader is celebrated for results, but people and posterity will never forget how those results were arrived at. You must discipline yourself to be able to work with constituted authority and within the rules, even while you push for change.**

The following statements are quite useful for you as an Emerging Leader. They will help you understand your level of determination to succeed. You should answer these questions grading from 1 to 5 where 1 is "not determined at all" and 5 is "ready to fight till I drop,"

- I will break the back of the most difficult situation I am faced with [Score]
- I will give of myself to the resolution of issues affecting others [score]
- I will achieve all that is expected of me [score]
- I will exceed all expectations, especially the ones I have of myself [score]
- I will make a lasting impression in my area of assignment [score]

Now, having discovered the desire for leadership that burns in your heart and also drummed up the determination to be the best and most impactful version of yourself possible, there is yet another trait you must look to build – and this is the discipline to see the journey through.

THE PRICE OF DISCIPLINE

Discipline is the combination of mental and emotional strength that enables a leader to work within self-imposed restraint in order to achieve a desired outcome. Effectively, discipline is the self-regulation required by every Emerging Leader who is determined to deliver excellence as a minimum standard. Discipline is a powerful tool for leaders – both in fair weather and difficult periods. It is the strength required to stay on track when things are not going as planned. It is also the strength required to remain focused when success is followed by a plethora of options for the leader to choose from. Discipline is a key hallmark of leaders who reach the height of their effectiveness and continuously stay relevant at that height.

Discipline is the force of self-control that enables you as an Emerging Leader to follow through on your stated goals. In the journey of any Emerging Leader, especially where there is early success, it is quite easy to lose focus and get sucked in with the trappings that come with success. This is best illustrated in the world of sport, where there are many young "superstars" enjoying the benefits and wealth their talent brings. For every talented and focused leader who stays the course and makes an impact, there is at least one other who does not quite make the grade – due to a lack of discipline. There are also others who regularly flatter to deceive, neither succeeding nor failing outright. In recent years in the English Premier League, footballers such as Steven Gerrard, Rio Ferdinand and David Beckham have been celebrated – not just for their talent, but for the discipline and application they consistently exhibited through many years of playing the game at the highest level. There are however too many individuals who started out with these men [and who were seen as equally talented] but were unable to focus enough to become all that they were expected to become.

In the Investment Banking and Wealth Management system – where I have served for well over a decade, a key theme that all leaders have to deal with is the directive to deliver effective and efficient service within specified constraints of schedule, budget and resource. The mantra usually is "do more with less." While this might sound like a terribly unfair expectation, I have found that the best leaders view these situations as the perfect opportunity to discipline themselves – challenge themselves to work within the set confines. These leaders are not afraid to confront the questions posed each day by the prevailing circumstances. These are the people who make a difference. As an Emerging Leader, you must understand that your mettle will always be tested by unfavourable situations and circumstances. **True leadership finds its expression in the midst of challenge and pressure.** As it is often said, *the purest diamond is born out of the greatest pressure.* Remember, you are not a leader because of your title- "Executive Director" or "Group Managing Director." You are a leader when you are able to apply discipline – first to yourself and then to the people and processes around you - in order to keep yourself, your team and your organisation on track for a specific outcome.

For Emerging Leaders who are young [in age, experience or knowledge]; it is important to note that many will look to you to be the voice agitating for change, even if you are not quite the change-maker yet. As you may well be aware, it is almost expected of youths to kick, protest or even rebel against constituted authority and established traditions. Indeed, many experienced leaders made their names on the "battlefields" of protest. However, being the loudest and the most outspoken person in the room is not necessarily the key to effecting change. As important as it may be to seek positive change, you owe it to yourself and to those who believe in you to stay on the right side of the law. This means you must have enough discipline to curb any excesses that are caused by your passion for change. Ultimately, a leader is celebrated for results, but people and posterity will never forget how those results were arrived at. You must discipline yourself to be able to work with constituted authority and within the rules, even while you push for change. It is so much more satisfying when you successfully challenge the status quo without breaking the law. **Too many would-be leaders have achieved short-term popularity and succumbed to long-term obscurity because of a lack of discipline**. Whatever you do, do not join this unfortunate statistic.

Examine - Equip - Emerge

Emerging Leaders must ask themselves the following questions:

Desire, Dedication, Discipline

1. Desire is a powerful force of the human mind that is manifested as a deep longing for a specific outcome. What specific outcomes do you have a deep-rooted longing to deliver and experience?

   ....
   ....
   ....
   ....
   ....

2. A leader's desire to lead is often in an ongoing battle with various factors that appear to limit his capacity or ability to do so. What battles have you faced [or are you facing] as you push ahead with your growth as a leader?

   ....
   ....
   ....
   ....
   ....

3. What advantages can you get as an Emerging Leader from understanding the concept of desire?

   ....
   ....

....

....

....

4. The challenges faced by leaders in today's world are multi-dimensional. How important is "determination" to you in your quest to deliver value in your chosen area of work?

    ....

    ....

    ....

    ....

    ....

5. What is the key difference between determination and stubborn foolhardiness?

    ....

    ....

    ....

    ....

    ....

6. When difficult situations come your way, what methods of self-discipline do you resort to and how have they helped you?

    ....

    ....

....

....

....

7. If you had to advise a colleague about the importance of discipline, which inspirational leader would you use as an example?

....

....

....

....

....

....

Talent without discipline is like an octopus on roller skates. There's plenty of movement, but you never know if it's going to be forward, backwards, or sideways.
-H. Jackson Brown Jr.

Creativity & Innovation

In the beginning, God created the heavens and the earth
- Genesis 1:1

L eadership - by definition is much more than keeping things ticking along smoothly (management takes care of that quite nicely). Leaders are expected to be the creators of the new reality, the initiators of the new knowledge and the front-runners who break through new frontiers. Your CV as a leader should talk about what was not - that you created or that you contributed to its emergence. Simply put, the "creator-leader" is typically the most impactful and most remembered.

> **Creativity is a trait that all leaders must have in their make-up. This is because the new reality that they are responsible for often does not exist yet.**

Creativity is a trait that all leaders must have in their make-up. This is because the new reality that they are responsible for often does not exist yet. Once the Emerging Leaders use their powers of imagination to travel into the desired future, they have the initial responsibility of relaying the vision of a better future to those who follow them. Over and above this, they have the responsibility of delivering the new reality - ensuring that the hope of a better future manifests as an eventual reality.

The late Dr. Nelson Mandela was a leader with a vision for a new reality in South Africa; a country without the racial discrimination that prevailed with minority rule. He did not just relay the vision to the people; he committed his life to bringing the new reality to manifestation. Dr. Mandela became President of his country and even in death still serves as a point of reference when issues of freedom and equal opportunities are discussed across the world.

The bible tells the story of Moses - a man who, thousands of years after his death is still a larger-than-life influence on Christianity and Judaism. Moses came to his people with a vision of a better tomorrow - one without the Egyptian slave masters and free from oppression. Moses lived all his years leading the Israelites to the "promised land" despite many hiccups and detours along the way.

Beatrice Mtetwa, a renowned human rights lawyer in Zimbabwe was born as the oldest daughter amongst more than 50 children. She worked her way in life based on the encouragement received from her teacher as well as a deeply entrenched desire to be the voice against oppression. These driving forces enabled her to convert her life hardship into a mission to help the defenceless who needed defending. In her quest to defend the rights of lawyers and the media, she has been arrested, beaten and tried in court for spurious allegations. Ms. Mtetwa remains a force that is changing institutionalised oppression in her country and has been recognised by numerous international organisations; including awards for ethical leadership and for creating measurable improvement in the lives and conditions of people.

As an Emerging Leader, much like the leaders listed above, it is true that the proof of your leadership is in the impactful and sustainable change you are able to create. As you emerge daily into your place of leadership, you will indeed find that although people may initially take your stated vision at face value, they will watch and wait to see whether there is any substance to your claims.

> **When a leader catches the vision that a better situation is required, he or she goes through a virtual experience of the changed world.**

CREATIVITY IS THE KEY COMPONENT OF CHANGE. Change is the key to effective leadership. This means that creativity is essential to leadership - and is not merely a flavour of leadership. There should be no meaningless differentiation of "creative leaders" from other leaders. It is after all the responsibility of leaders to directly create or indirectly influence the creation of the shift from the status quo to the experience of a new reality.

> **Conscious acceptance of any challenge is crucial to the effectiveness of a leader**

To fully understand the concept and impact of creativity, so that you as an Emerging Leader can fully tap into this core of your leadership responsibility, we must take a step back to the leadership activity that precedes the delivery of what is created.

CREATIVITY CHAIN

1. Creativity starts for all leaders in the mind. Creativity is predicated by the experience of the new reality that the leader

has been through in his or her imagination. When a leader catches the vision that a better situation is required, he or she goes through a virtual experience of the changed world. This plays out differently for the individual leader, but always happens. This individual experience is what generates the conviction in the mind of the leader and fires up the belief that makes them assume responsibility for delivering the change. You can probably relate to a change that you have imagined and taken responsibility for - whether as a student, an up-and-coming professional or an established leader. The strength of your conviction as a leader is a function of the vividness of the future picture that you have seen.

2. The second step in the "creativity process" that leaders go through is **accepting the challenge of creativity**. From the small easy-to-achieve quick win to the profoundly impossible-to-fathom change, leaders must accept the challenge to create or influence the creation of change. If the challenge is not fully accepted, there is the possibility of "leader's fatigue" part way through the journey of change and this can eventually grind the change to a halt. I have had personal experiences of changes where I accepted the creativity challenge for - and successfully delivered. I have also struggled in accepting some creativity challenge and delivering on them. Conscious acceptance of any challenge is crucial to the effectiveness of a leader [even if the acceptance is reluctantly done]. This is much more so where the challenge involves creating something new. Creativity demands that the leader is ready to go up against all odds and constraints.

3. The third step in the "creativity process" that leaders go through is the **breaking down of barriers to progress**. As earlier

mentioned, all leaders should expect to come up against some forces of resistance as they serve out their leadership purpose. This is because leadership by definition is a double-barrelled activity of discovering the need for change and delivering the impact of change. As an Emerging Leader, you will encounter resistance to your ideas or your work at some stage in your career. You will find yourself beset by what I will refer to as the "strongholds of opposition".

> **Ultimately, you must make the choice to either push ahead or abandon the ship – irrespective of the opposition you face from those who are close to you.**

STRONGHOLDS OF OPPOSITION

There are two broad types of opposition - **extrinsic** and **intrinsic**.

EXTRINSIC OPPOSITION

Extrinsic opposition to creativity refers to the resistance or challenge that comes from external sources. These are usually from persons, teams or organisations that may not fully understand your idea or may be somewhat threatened by what you intend to do. It is also possible that extrinsic opposition comes from systems that are not even aware of you or your idea. Extrinsic opposition may come in a variety of guises, including:

MANAGEMENT: You exercise your leadership mind-set by identifying an issue and proposing a solution – but the team management put the brakes on your idea. I had the potential conflict between leadership and management brought home to me when as a young test analyst in an international organisation; I spotted gaps in the team's reporting system. My fledgling leadership instinct immediately led me to documenting the issue and proposing a solution that would require an adventurous mind-set to implement. What took me the better part of two weeks to document and present took less than two minutes for my manager to dismantle and dismiss. As far as she could see, there was no need for the level of change I was proposing and I would do well to focus my attention on the business of the day – running test scripts. I was quite disappointed, but the episode taught me a valuable lesson on how to handle this type of setbacks.

FAMILY, FRIENDS AND PEERS: You have a dream of doing something big, changing your world or delivering significant value – and in your excitement, you share the dream with members of your family. Like most people you expect unflinching support and understanding from brothers, sisters and parents. To your great shock, you get a combination of lukewarm apathy and outright disapproval. The bible tells the story of a young man called Joseph, who narrated his dreams to his family only to face strong waves of ill-feeling that led to his brothers trading him into slavery. This might sound like an extreme situation, but as a Coach, I once had a client who spoke to me outside of our coaching agreement - requesting independent advice on the business idea he was developing. This client claimed that as much as he believed that his plans were on the right path, he had failed to convince the two most important persons in his life [his wife and his bosom friend of over 15 years] to support him. Effectively, the key support areas he depended on in his bid to create something, had let him down.

As an Emerging Leader you must be prepared to either enjoy

support or experience resistance from members of your family or your circle of friends. How you deal with such resistance will go some way in determining how well you will do in the "lonely place" that leaders occupy. Ultimately, you must make the choice to either push ahead or abandon the ship – irrespective of the opposition you face from those who are close to you.

GOVERNMENT AND GOVERNING SYSTEMS: As an Emerging Leader, you must be acquainted with systems that govern your area of operation. These systems are driven and administered by various laws, rules and regulations – which you are expected to work with. This will apply whether you are employed within an organisation or you operate as a "free-lance" consultant. Failure to operate within stated regulatory guidelines and laws usually attracts high penalties. For instance, the banking and finance industry was heavily regulated before the global financial crisis of 2008. The crisis has led to a further tightening of the regulatory framework that guides the industry. Against this backdrop, you must remain a leader seeking to create in order to deliver change and add value. Without setting out to directly oppose your ideas, the increasingly stringent regulatory environment could stand as an obstacle to your creativity.

> Since the mind is the birthplace of your imaginative powers as a leader, it makes sense to return to your imagination to achieve a turnaround of the opposition. This can be done either privately or with the help of a professional.

As an Emerging Leader, it is imperative that you gain good understanding of the regulatory and legal frameworks that govern your area of operation. It is also important that you do not allow these frameworks to stifle your idea or creativity. **The most effective leaders are those who can apply their creativity within the boundaries of the regulations.**

INTRINSIC OPPOSITION

This refers to opposing forces within the leader himself. The leader, inadvertently, sets up barriers that hinder his progress. Intrinsic opposition to creativity is potentially more damaging that extrinsic opposition. This is because it is driven from the command centre of the leader – the mind. As many great leadership practitioners have taught, the leader's mind is the most potent limiting force he can face. In other words, the person with the greatest power and opportunity to derail your creativity is **you**! There are a number of reasons why leaders may suffer intrinsic opposition to creativity, including:

- **FEAR OF FAILURE -** this makes leaders unable to release their creativity because of an irrational and sometimes uncontrollable fear that they might not get things quite right. Fear of failure creates in leaders, a feeling of self-doubt and typically manifests as a disinclination or reluctance to undertake activity that they otherwise would. Fear of failure is detrimental to creativity as it negates the instinct to pursue change. Taking the first step to creativity becomes a herculean and unwanted challenge.

- **FEAR OF SUCCESS -** the leader experiences a sense of apprehension related to the successful delivery of change. He wants the change but he is afraid of it. Although this fear affects people differently, it generally relates to the fear of change itself. For an Emerging Leader whose stock in trade is all about change, this is quite a daunting fear. Quite a number of questions bug the minds of leaders who experience this fear. For no apparent reason the leader becomes apprehensive about the aftermath of success, the possibility of things going wrong after the crest of the wave has been ridden, as well as coping with increased expectations that result from success. This fear stifles creativity and even causes self-sabotage in leaders.

· **FEAR OF REJECTION** - Anyone who has championed change or created something new would be somewhat acquainted with the fear of rejection. The desire for acceptance comes as part of the package of the creative spirit that a leader possesses – after all, nobody wants to invest time and life in creating what will not be acceptable. For some leaders however, the fear of rejection is so pronounced that it forms a barrier to their ability to press forward and deliver the change they have committed to. This intrinsic opposition creeps up on the blind side of the leader [leaders tend to think positively and can be guilty of not taking any negative vibes or emotions into consideration]. Leaders affected by this fear tend to procrastinate – putting off activity related to creativity in the hope that doing nothing will reduce the risk of rejection. The net effect is that work stagnates and the leader experiences feelings of inadequacy and low self-esteem [arising from the rejection that has not happened].

As an Emerging Leader, dealing with intrinsic opposition to creativity will be a much greater challenge than dealing with any extrinsic opposition can be. This is because you effectively have to fight yourself to save yourself! There are some effective strategies that you can deploy in order to fight off intrinsic opposition to creativity.

COMBATING INTRINSIC OPPOSITION

- **Reverse the "what if" question**– All intrinsic opposition to creativity feeds off a "what if" question. What if I fail? What if I get it wrong? What if I cannot cope with success? What if people expect more than I can give? What if the Management Board refuses to accept my work? Once the leader becomes anxious about the answer to the first "what if" question, the mind comes up with many more, and then with more sinister variations of the same questions – locking the leader in a never-ending spiral of fear. Reversing each "what if" question to its positive opposite is an effective way of dealing with this situation. Instead of "what if I fail?" ask "what if I succeed?" Instead of "what if I get it wrong?" ask "what if I get it right?" Instead of "what if the Management Board refuses to accept my work?" ask "what if the Management Board is excited about my work?" As an emerging Leader

> Not trying is not an option. Giving up is also not an option. At the end of the day, the leader who makes change happen will believe the impossible and expend some effort to ensure the switch from impossible to possible.

going up against the power of your own mind, you will find that controlling the "argument" in this manner can be quite effective.

· **Return to the root of creativity [imagination]** – The key to breaking the stronghold of intrinsic opposition to creativity is getting back control of the mind. Since the mind is the birthplace of your imaginative powers as a leader, it makes sense to return to your imagination to achieve a turnaround of the opposition. This can be done either privately or with the help of a professional. Should you find your path to creativity blocked by intrinsically driven forces, you will need to trace your way back to the new reality you imagined at the start of the creative process.

· **Get the support of coaches, mentors and teachers** – As an Emerging Leader, it is imperative that you surround yourself with a network of coaches, teachers and mentors that you consider worthy of trust and are experienced enough to serve as your sounding board or counsellor. It is often said that no one succeeds in isolation. I have had the privilege of speaking with coaches and mentors whenever I was faced with challenging times through my career. It is however important to note that they may not take ownership of your problem or carry your burden, but their input in terms of advice, comfort and guidance can go a long way in snapping you out of negative situations.

INNOVATION

Innovation focuses more on bringing the force of change to what already exists. Innovation is considered to be **a product of the creativity trait** – the key difference being that "**Organic Creativity**" is seen to start from what never existed [develop a product, process, service that no one has offered before]. For instance, researching and developing a drug that cures an ailment previously believed to be incurable.

"**Innovative Creativity**" - or innovation - on the other hand, is the process of renewal – bringing significant change or turnaround to an existing product, process or service. This may include improvements to specific attributes of a product or service that enables clients or customers to view the product or service in a new light – translating to a marked improvement in sales, profit or customer goodwill.

Some research into innovation as an organisational culture indicates that up to 75% of leaders surveyed considered innovation as either not an important part – or at best an informal inclusion - of the strategic planning process. This apparent lack of organisational innovation, in many instances is traced to a lack of innovative thinking on the part of the individual leaders who are responsible for the direction of the organisation. The individual leadership traits of an organisation's command centre will have a major impact on the collective direction of that organisation. If you are to make the desired difference in your organisation, you will need to display strength in innovative thinking – and be an **active encourager** of innovative creativity. You need the drive to see change, as well as the courage to implement the change.

It is therefore important that as a leader emerging daily into your place of service delivery, you have an understanding of innovation and how it can become a platform for the establishment of your leadership legacy. Leaders who do not leave their mark or impact on their area of assignment are likely to be written off as "light weight" or ineffectual leaders. Creating new out of the old is one sure fire way of leaving your mark. It does not matter whether you do this in an effective, slow burning manner [akin to incremental innovation] or you hit the ground running strongly against the tide and deliver quick, instantly recognisable change [akin to radical innovation]. What does matter at the end of the day is your delivery of ground breaking change – for which your organisation or community will be better off.

What we all understand as leaders in the 21st century is that we operate in an increasingly challenging, unpredictable and demanding environment. There are new situations on a daily – even hourly – basis that require something different as a solution. There are many tried and tested solutions to leadership problems; some have repeatedly failed the test of time and are no longer effective. There is also a palpable vacuum in the ongoing "master process" of innovative creativity – perhaps due to a prevalent misunderstanding amongst Emerging Leaders that the spirit of innovative creativity is inferior to the spirit of organic creativity. Leaders are too quick to discard the possibility of improving existing products and processes – citing cost and aggressive change environment as their reasons. As a result, they overlook opportunities to innovate in favour of chasing dreams of "absolute originality." I encourage you as an Emerging Leader to give your ability to innovate as many chances as your ability to originate. As a leader myself, I am intrigued and fascinated by the biblical account of the six days of creation – a mix of organic and innovative creativity by the Master of the universe himself.

The innovative emerging leader is one who is not afraid to ask the probing, difficult, offbeat and sometimes provocative questions of the current way of doing things. Not that they will refuse to do things using the current method, they will simply see questions on how various stages of the existing process operates, and with the questions, they generally come up with proposals for change. This is because their approach to thinking about the process does not give preference to the current method – thereby not relying on the known facts as a base; rather their thinking is based on what better way is possible. This intuitive, courageous and instinctive thinking gives innovative creativity its relevance. As an Emerging Leader, you owe it to yourself, your family, your community, your organization, your nation, and any individual who directly or indirectly depends on the product of your mind – to free up your thinking so that you can produce your best results for the improvement of those around you.

As I conclude this chapter, I encourage you as Emerging Leaders – whether inclined towards organic or innovative creativity – to always have faith in the "possibility of better." Your role as a leader will more often than not challenge the current understanding. Even when some of the products of your mind do not initially make the desired or required impact, you will need to believe enough to continue with your experimentation, probing and challenging. Not trying is not an option. Giving up is also not an option. At the end of the day, the leader who makes change happen will believe the impossible and expend some effort to ensure the switch from impossible to possible. I leave you with a few questions that can get you into the groove of, or stay on track with your creativity.

Examine – Equip - Emerge

Creativity and Innovation

1. Which existing gap in your current reality can you bridge by virtue of your skill, ability, knowledge or resources?

   ....
   ....
   ....
   ....
   ....

2. How do you intend to tackle the responsibility you have as a leader for delivering value-added change through creativity?

   ....
   ....
   ....
   ....
   ....

3. What obstacles stand in the way of your creativity and what do you intend to do about them?

   ....
   ....
   ....
   ....
   ....

4. What can you see around you that works today but can work better either today or in the future?

    ....
    ....
    ....
    ....
    ....

5. How often do you employ new ways of getting things done without discarding the existing tools or processes?

    ....
    ....
    ....
    ....

6. How prepared would you say you are for the initial negative reaction to your ideas?

    ....
    ....
    ....
    ....
    ....

7. Creativity is essential to leadership. What are you creating or have created that excites you as a leader?

    ....
    ....

....

....

....

8. In your journey as a leader, how have you dealt with intrinsic opposition to your creativity?

....

....

....

....

....

We cannot solve a problem by using the same kind of
thinking we used when we created them.
- Albert Einstein

chapter 8

Teachable & Learning Spirit

"Leadership and learning are indispensable to each other."

— John F. Kennedy

Many of the desirable and important traits of Emerging Leaders in this book have also been published in several thousands of books by great teachers. There is however a character trait that can – and regularly will – become the making or breaking of an Emerging Leader. This is the Emerging Leader's attitude to, and aptitude for learning. The attitude part forms the basis of the Emerging Leader's *"teachability"*, while 'aptitude' refers to the Emerging Leader's *"spirit of learning"*.

Learning is not an optional activity for leaders; indeed, learning is not an optional activity for life. It is a well-accepted understanding that as long as life continues, learning continues – the process of death starts with the rejection or cessation of learning. Choosing not to learn from experience or from others is the singularly most dangerous decision any leader can make; it is the decision that renders their leadership irrelevant and of no consequence to the area they were meant to impact.

As an Emerging Leader, your commitment to learning is your

commitment to continued relevance in the community, organisation or marketplace in which you operate. **Learning is the cornerstone of leadership.** The importance of learning to leadership cannot be overstated. We live and operate in a world that consists of many convoluted and inter-connected systems. Although, these systems were intended by design to provide order and predictability to organisations and communities, these systems are in a constant state of unpredictable movements and therefore, unstable. The level of instability of the world systems can range from mild movement to uncontrollable turbulence. Your leadership will be tested and expected to deliver results against this backdrop.

What is also quite interesting is the increasing pace at which change is practically "inflicted" by these systems on the things and positions that we know. There is barely enough time to become familiar or conversant with one way of doing things before the next "big thing" arrives and renders the existing method obsolete. It is almost impossible to predict the pace of change and predetermine the learning that must be maintained in order to keep up with change – let alone stride ahead of the pace of change. What is known though, is that the cost of rejecting, delaying or even simply undercooking the learning that an Emerging Leader undergoes is increasingly higher and more profoundly destructive than ever before. The collapse of huge multinationals such as Enron and Lehmann Brothers during the recent financial crisis points to the magnitude of impact that can result from a failure to learn from experience.

It is pertinent that we define in this chapter what learning really is. Despite many excellent pieces of research into learning by scholars over the last few decades, there is still a critically lame understanding of the meaning and process of learning – especially as it pertains to leadership. Learning is the completion of an end-to-end process that results in impactful and evidential delivery of change or transformation to an existing entity. This means that learning is not the same thing as the gathering of new or modified information, but rather an overarching process that encompasses the formal and informal gathering of information and culminates in the utilisation of that information to affect the environment, community, organisation, government, nation or indeed global governing systems. The *"Five A's of Learning"* describe this repeatable process.

> You are responsible for managing your continued learning and as such, you will need to gain access to the information required to keep you up to speed with changes in your area of operation – and to give you a platform to move ahead of the competition.

FIVE A's OF LEARNING

1. **ACKNOWLEDGE THE NEED FOR LEARNING** – This is the first stage of learning where you as an Emerging Leader become aware of a "body of knowledge" that is currently unavailable to you. At this stage, you also become consciously accepting of the need to acquire that knowledge. This may be linked to the need to resolve a particular situation that you are faced with and an associated acceptance that some knowledge or experience is missing. This could also

come as a direct result of failure in a specific area of your work or other area of life [it has been suggested that failure is one of the most effective motivators of learning]. Working closely with a teacher, life or business coach, mentor or trusted advisor may also help you acknowledge the need for knowledge. It is important to note that this stage is not completed simply because someone says to you that some learning is required. It must be the case that you as an Emerging Leader internally and consciously arrive at the point where acquiring that knowledge becomes a need; **the point where hunger for knowledge is linked to a strong desire to achieve a purpose-driven goal**. Once the knowledge in question is no longer a "nice-to-have", you will find yourself with a desire so strong for the knowledge that you will be mentally and physically prepared for the next step in learning. In one of my early testing roles in a major investment bank, I quickly realised that I absolutely needed to understand the account opening process [I was responsible for testing account feeds

> **Your attitude to knowledge acquisition will feed into how well you can make use of the knowledge that you do acquire.**

from the system's backend]. This was to enable me resolve issues that were found with the feeds – and resolve them from a position of knowledge. I was not required by my job description to know the account opening process – it was a call for increased value from within me to pursue that learning. I can write today that it was quite beneficial to myself and the team that I picked up that knowledge.

2. **ACCESS THE REQUIRED INFORMATION** – The next stage of learning is a search activity – aimed at gaining access to the data, information or knowledge that has previously been identified as a need. The importance of getting access to the right information cannot be overemphasized. In my career as a business coach, I have come across many clients who are increasingly frustrated at their lack of access to information. This may sound strange considering the apparent overflow of information available on the Internet and across different media. My observation is that it is one thing to have information stored all over the place – and quite another thing for those who require the information to gain access to it.

> **You must learn to trust your instincts – which in any case are a partial product of your experience.**

As an Emerging Leader, you are responsible for managing your continued learning and as such, you will need to gain access to the information required to keep you up to speed with changes in your area of operation – and to give you a platform to move ahead of the competition. Access to the right information at the right time is important for all leaders, regardless of level of experience or area of operation. Gaining access can be challenging due to the cost [for example, fees payable to an institution for training]. Other challenges to gaining access to information may include time [organising your schedule to ensure you are prepared to take in time-sensitive information] and availability [for instance, required courses being over-subscribed]. Whatever the challenge, this is a stage of learning that every leader must deal with successfully.

3. **ACQUIRE THE KNOWLEDGE** – Once access to the required information has been obtained, your next move as a leader is to actually acquire the information. This may be done in a number of ways, including attending formal training courses at institutions or through web-based training offerings, spending time in self-learning through online study, learning "on-the-job" by working with experienced colleagues and reviewing your own past efforts to learn from mistakes and establish good practices.

> **Your legacy will be built each day based on how you choose to utilise the information you have, and what impact your use of that information has on the people who have expectations of you.**

As an Emerging Leader, it is important that you treat knowledge as a valuable acquisition – whether it is the simple "how-to" tip from an operation manual, the latest development in cutting-edge technology or highly important information to aid investment. Your attitude to knowledge acquisition will feed into how well you can make use of the knowledge that you do acquire. My observation as a business coach is that leaders who value knowledge highly are usually more effective at applying the acquired knowledge to problem resolution.

> **The more teachable a leader is, the more that leader will learn, know and deploy.**

4. **ANALYSE THE ACQUIRED INFORMATION** – as an Emerging Leader, a major key to making effective use of information lies in your ability to critically analyse the information that you receive. A critical analysis usually involves breaking the information down into content as well as attribute components. Your analysis should seek to discern what parts of the received information is useful for what purpose, how best to make use of the information, what impact the information could have on you, on the people around you and on the situations in which the information will be deployed.

> **They see new or better knowledge as opportunities to improve, rather than threats to the status quo.**

You should also consider whether to use any of the information or whether to discard it in its entirety. If the information turns out to have come from sources that are less than ideal or if the information has been delivered to encourage inappropriate behaviour, you should choose not to use it [for instance, illegally acquired insider information within a bank that could result in unfair trading]. The strength of your character will be tested when the rights or wrong of acquired information are not quite clear – and you have to make a call on whether or not to use it.

Simply put, the more you can find out about the information that comes your way, the better placed you are to act with appropriate discretion should you choose to use the information. The insight that comes from analysis also protects you as a leader from errors that can cause damage to your reputation or financial standing.

There are going to be times when your "analysis" of information will be limited to a few moments' brainwork. For instance, you are given information at an informal meeting that could lead to a business breakthrough; you have no access to your planning figures, but you have to make an instant decision to ward off potential competitors. In situations like these, you must learn to trust your instincts – which in any case are a partial product of your experience.

5. **ACTIVATE AND ACTUALISE** – Now that you have acquired and analysed the information, the final stage of the learning process is putting the knowledge to work – and making the right type of impact with it. This is where you stamp your signature on your work – and on the value that you deliver. The knowledge that you have access to – even that which you have a monopoly on, is dormant and of no effect until you "activate" that knowledge by applying it to problem resolution, individual or community education

or any other value-add activity. The real proof of learning is in what you do with the knowledge acquired.

The saying that "knowledge is power" will become particularly relevant to you as an Emerging Leader when you consider the responsibility that leadership places on you as well as the expectations that your friends, family, organisation or community will have of you. Responsibility and expectation are more often than not increased by your access to information. What you know only becomes power when it is applied. As an Emerging Leader, your legacy will be built each day based on how you choose to utilise the information you have, and what impact your use of that information has on the people who have expectations of you.

It is important that your use of information be within the confines and stipulations of the law. I am sure that you will have read of many leaders or persons in positions of responsibility who have lost the trust of their employers or clients through inappropriate or illegal use of information [my time in the Investment Banking and Wealth Management industry has been quite educational in this respect]. It is also of great importance that you stay on the side of decency and morality in your deployment of information in your professional and private life. As a leader, you owe it to yourself and those who place their trust in you to treat information with the respect and carefulness it deserves. Your rise or fall as an Emerging Leader could very well hinge on this.

It has been said quite often that those who want to be impactful as leaders, must be passionate about learning. The effective, legally sound and morally upright use of knowledge [otherwise known as "wisdom"] is a key differentiating factor between the "wannabe" leaders and those who actually leave their mark on their world through impactful leadership.

Now that we are armed with an understanding of the learning process, it is necessary to know how the concept of *"teachability"* affects the Emerging Leader and why it is important for any leader to be teachable. Teachability is the leadership trait that causes an Emerging Leader to passionately desire, discover and deploy knowledge as a precursor to delivering value. It is where the leader displays the required humility that admits ignorance in order to make the learning process complete. Teachability therefore, is superior to learning – it is the key that makes learning what it is. The more teachable a leader is, the more that leader will learn, know and deploy.

Teachability has more to do with your attitude as an Emerging Leader rather than your ability to learn. When a leader is not just "open" to learning, but actually has a passion for learning, it is much easier to realise their leadership potential. We have mentioned earlier in this book that our world – with its fast-moving, ever-changing variables, presents a challenge to all leaders. All leaders must be able to adapt to change quickly and proactively develop the skills and knowhow that is required to continuously deliver solutions.

As a youth development practitioner, I have had the pleasure of looking out for young men and women in the local community churches that I have been affiliated with. From when I started out in 1996 through 2016, there has been a variety of changes to laws regarding youth working, a catalogue of changes to the technology available to young persons; as well as differences in the way parents relate to children and how youth workers relate to both parents and children. Through all of these, I have been keen to learn whatever new idea or method that became available – especially if it could make me a better youth leader. I would attend youth conventions and meet up with other youth development practitioners like myself – all with a spark in their eyes – looking forward to sharing ideas and learning off each other.

Leaders with a teachable spirit are those who have such faith in their leadership ability and purpose, that they are not threatened by the knowledge available to other persons or groups. They see new or better knowledge as opportunities to improve, rather than threats to the status quo. Such leaders are able to accord the required respect to the owners or carriers of new information. This makes the teachable leaders more effective in a competitive market place. In a market where a skilful mix of flexibility and stability is required, the teachable leader comes out a winner repeatedly. This is because they are able to stand true to their own principles, whilst recognising the potential benefits that new knowledge can bring to them. For instance, looking at the very competitive social media market, the leading lights such as Facebook are able to stay ahead of the pack by having a positive attitude to learning; many others have found growth less easy to come by – partially because they have not been as welcoming to newer ways of doing things.

A high level of teachability in an Emerging Leader is crucial to the growth of that leader. Growth in its purest form is a function of learning and experience. The teachable leaders value each experience they go through – "banking" such experiences as part of their growth, and in many cases, looking forward to the next experience – even if that experience involves some "growth pains". A serial and successful entrepreneur I know once confessed to me that he would not be anywhere near as successful as he was, if he was not prepared to learn in the rough as well as smooth times. The teachable leader can be said to have a "love for learning" that is stronger than the need to appear learned. This strong affinity for learning moves such leaders to search that little bit deeper below the surface when seeking information – thereby having the ability to make more of information than other leaders.

In summary, teachability and learning affinity are differentiating traits that enhance the leader's ability to exert influence effectively. As an Emerging Leader, you should ask yourself the following questions – so you can understand your attitude to learning and its impact on your effectiveness as a leader.

Examine – Equip - Emerge

Teachable and Learning Spirit - Chapter 8

1. What makes you more excited and why - the opportunity to learn, or the actual process of learning?

   ....
   ....
   ....
   ....
   ....

2. Could you estimate what percentage of the information you have taken in over the last 12 months that you have put into effective use?

   ....
   ....
   ....
   ....
   ....

3. On a scale of 1 to 5 [where 1 is "highly embarrassing" and 5 is "not embarrassing at all"] how would you score being taught by a junior colleague on basic things you ought to have known?

   ....
   ....
   ....
   ....
   ....

4. How would you advise a colleague who is reluctant to undertake a training programme that is aimed at lower grades in the organization?

    ....
    ....
    ....
    ....
    ....

5. How have you worked to provide a resolution to a problem that you were not equipped with the right knowledge to resolve?

    ....
    ....
    ....
    ....
    ....

6. Teachability is more about your attitude to learning than your ability to learn. How "teachable" would you say you are? In what way has your teachability helped you as an Emerging Leader?

    ....
    ....
    ....
    ....

7. What strategies have you used to improve your knowledge? Do the five "A"s of Learning represent a process you would look to follow?

....

....

....

....

....

"Learning is not attained by force.
It must be sought for with ardour and diligence."
— Abigail Adams

Accountability

A ccountability is the acknowledgement and acceptance of responsibility for all actions rendered and decisions made as part of service delivery – including the impact [direct or otherwise] of such actions and decisions. Accountability goes beyond the reporting of activity [giving an account]. Accountability is taking ownership of the pre-activity expectations, the activity itself as well as the post-activity fall-out. As an Emerging Leader, your effectiveness is determined by the measurable change or transformation you either facilitate or directly deliver. Whenever your activity results in change or transformation of anything, you must be prepared to be accountable for the results and their associated impact.

Effective leadership and accountability are inseparable – you cannot have one without the other. Through my career as a coach and trainer, I have had the privilege of working with leaders from a variety of backgrounds and in a variety of

> **Irrespective of what the outcome looks like, leaders must be courageous and self-respecting, and must not hide away from the consequences.**

industries. One of the common traits I found in those who were either already successful, or have since achieved success, was their willingness to step up and be accountable to stakeholders – including senior management, peers, team members, clients and even themselves – for the outcomes of their actions. Irrespective of what the outcome looks like, leaders must be courageous and self-respecting, and must not hide away from the consequences. As my father on a few occasions said to me "if you can take the applause when things go well, you must be man enough to face the music when things do not go so well".

As an Emerging Leader, accountability keeps you grounded and honest. It enables you to look inward – reviewing your own performance in every situation, and ensuring that you never drop your levels of performance. Accountability prevents you from pointing the finger of blame at every available opportunity. This is one of the key strengths that can be found in leaders who are known for building effective teams and getting the best out of them. I have sat through hundreds of recruitment interview hours and I can testify that the most attractive organisations to work for are those that place a high value on teamwork. These organisations in turn are actively seeking team builders who encourage rather than blame - people who are able to deal with the weight of responsibility and accountability.

As a perennial student of leadership, I am continuously performing informal studies on groups of leaders in diverse industries. One such study was on Football coaches and managers in the major European leagues [Spain, Italy, England, Germany and France]. I found that across different countries, the managers who have won multiple trophies and built strong teams, are those who do not find it convenient to blame the weather, the state of the football pitch, the referee, the referee's assistant or even the opposing team for anything that goes wrong. Successful managers such as Sir Alex Ferguson and Josep Guardiola have been described as perfectionists – with the desire to improve themselves acting as a driving force in the character development of the players in the team. In like manner, as an Emerging Leader, you must always ask yourself questions that check how well you are doing, what you can do better, what you should do more of, what you should do less of, what you should start doing and what you should stop doing – tasking yourself to be more accountable for your thoughts and actions.

In all my travels, I am yet to meet a leader who has never made a mistake. As it is said, "stuff happens". However, the odd bad result or negative feedback should not be an invitation for you as an Emerging Leader to engage yourself in a moaning or self-pity session. In the same vein, your successes should not be an invitation for outrageous or over-the-top celebrations. You need a sense of perspective in all situations. Ideally, you should view your actions and the attendant results as a continuum of causes and effects – all of which add to your

> **"there is more than one I in accountability".** History and research continually show that in teams, organisations and communities where accountability is not woven into the culture fabric, the rate of growth – if any – will be quite slow.

experience as a leader. Good and bad results alike should trigger a self-assessment within you that is aimed at improvement in your next delivery. This is how leaders increase in their ability to add value to their organisations or teams. Regardless of the situation, leaders must remain accountable for their actions – in whichever facet of life their actions pertain to. Every time I have seen people who singularly take the plaudits when good times are abound but resort to apportioning blame when times are not as good – I have observed that they lack the character that underpins effective leadership. A very useful key to impactful leadership is being able to manage the impact of your results, first on yourself and then on others.

As an Emerging Leader you are always going to be a part of a team or other community based work group. Within such group structures, members will have corporate or joint accountability for certain work-packages or outcomes. They may also have individual responsibility for lower-level tasks within those work packages. As an individual in a team, the importance of your accountability within that group cannot be over-emphasised. A good response to the popular saying *"there is no I in team"*, should be *"there is more than one I in accountability"*. History and research continually show that in teams, organisations and communities where accountability is not woven into the culture fabric, the rate of growth – if any – will be quite slow. Whatever else we say about teams and the *"sum of their individual parts"*, the facts remain that these individual parts are essential in the making of a team – and need to be functioning at full tilt in order to produce an excellent team. Functioning at full tilt includes setting goals, planning activities that will help the team achieve the goals and accepting individual as well as corporate accountability for the success or failure of any work done. Simply put, accountability in leaders is crucial to organisational growth.

Organisations need leaders who are aware of the pressure that comes with being accountable – and yet are willing to accept accountability as individuals where necessary and as part of the group. Organisations grow through learning – and it is essential that the leaders drive this culture of learning. A lack of leaders who are accountable makes it quite difficult for organisations to understand the errors of the past and put improvement plans in place. In teams where leaders and followers are not willing to be held accountable for the success or failure of undertaken work, deepening levels of mediocrity will creep in until a culture of low quality and multiple excuses is created. As an Emerging Leader, it is important that you are not instrumental in creating the wrong atmosphere in the workplace. Indeed, your attitude of accountability should serve as a positive example to your colleagues in the team or organisation.

Accountability is a very important trait found only in leaders who are committed

> **Your accountability levels will affect the people who deliver the service, as well as those who seek to benefit from or experience the service.**

> **Seek clarity on goals you have been set, be clear on the goals that you set for yourself and also ensure you understand the expectations of your clients.**

to the delivery of excellence and also to upholding high standards of service delivery. In an ideal world, these would be the only type of leaders available. As an Emerging Leader, you should have the accountability trait as a naturally occurring one – or work hard to grow yourself to the level where it becomes a part of your core. It is vital that as you grow through to leadership maturity, you do not "go-easy" on yourself when it comes to issues concerning accountability. Holding yourself accountable is much more important to leadership development than being held accountable from the "outside". When you develop this trait in yourself, you are able to combat and conquer the tendency to give excuses for performances that are below expectations; you are also able to dispassionately review situations and move into problem-solving mode much quicker than leaders with a weaker sense of accountability.

In organisations where accountability levels have slipped, it can be difficult to pinpoint how and when the slide started. However, a common sight in such organisations is the tendency for senior managers to tolerate performance or activity that is slightly below expectation – for instance late delivery of work, correct content with poor presentation, simple office etiquette or even inappropriate communication standards. You may not find anyone openly encouraging poor performance, but the behaviour where accountability issues are not challenged quickly permeates the team or organisation. This "culture" of acceptance is a clear sign that individually and hence corporately, accountability levels are in need of a boost. As an Emerging Leader, if you find yourself in such an environment, it is imperative that you do not allow yourself slide along with lower expectations. You must hold yourself accountable for your actions and work deliveries at all times – as this is the source of your professional pride. It is quite possible that your attitude can kick-start the reversal of a culture that has threatened to engulf your team. Portraying a positive attitude going up against a negative culture can be challenging, but is one of the ways in which your leadership can be impactful in the workplace and the community.

As an Emerging Leader – whether you work on your own or as part of a team, your level of accountability will have an impact on the service delivered by the individual or the team. Your accountability levels will affect the people who deliver the service, as well as those who seek to benefit from or experience the service. Against this backdrop, it is not surprising to note how much importance and emphasis that organisations place on the issue of accountability. From internal training programmes to carefully worded corporate communications, many organisations are going "full-throttle" to ensure that staff and clients alike key into accountability as a core value. The potential damage to organisations are wide and far-reaching; hence much thought is put towards discovering and tackling the root causes of accountability failures. In my experience of working with and

> **A person who feels valued is better placed to step up and take on the mantle – and pressures – of accountability for delivery. By the same token, a person who feels more tolerated than valued will most likely be reluctant to take up accountability for task delivery.**

advising leaders, I have identified three of the most potent root causes of accountability failure – three root causes that you, as an Emerging Leader need to be aware of in order to deliver your best service all the time.

> **Leaders who will leave a mark in the sands of time are those who will overcome many obstacles to seize the mantle of accountability. These are the leaders who are not afraid of failure**

Unclear Responsibility – This is one of the most common causes of accountability failure in individuals and organisations. The "holy grail" of leadership is the conversion of expectations into manifested reality. However, when a leader is not clear about what is expected, she is starved of the key driving component of leadership. When this happens there is a tendency to either produce less than is the required standard or perhaps do more – but in the wrong direction. It is a quite simple reality – unclear goals and expectations lead to confusion and confusion in turn is the procreator of poor quality delivery. If you ever wondered why setting goals is so important to leaders or why the ever-popular S.M.A.R.T template for setting goals has stood the test of time since the 1980s, you only need to look at the number of failed businesses that cite poor planning, poorly communicated goals or a disconnect in understanding between the goal setters and the implementers. As an Emerging Leader, it is absolutely important that you seek clarity on goals you have been set, be clear on the goals that you set for yourself and also ensure you understand the expectations of your clients. It really does help you as a leader to know what you are accountable for and who you are accountable to. There is a popular saying that "knowledge is power". I would go further to say that "knowledge is the component that either makes power impactful or renders it completely useless".

Fear of Stretch Challenges–Another common root cause of accountability failure that Emerging Leaders need to be aware of is the "fear of stretch". This is the state of mind that leaders can fall into when faced with the prospect of work that will require more ability, knowledge or experience than is currently at their disposal. This may sound a strange thing to say about leaders [after all, are all leaders not "energized by pressure" and "thrive on challenges"?].

Experience tells us that most leaders are fully aware of the ability and experience that they possess and would recognise a stretch challenge once it is presented [whether that is stepping in for the team leader, working for a bigger client or even managing a bigger portfolio than is usual]. I have witnessed many leaders who are normally quite capable and effective at what they do – have a "wobble" when presented with the opportunity to be accountable for a stretch task. This fear of the stretch task can put leaders into a state of "delivery inertia" where they find it difficult to make any headway in the delivery of work that they have initially accepted to be accountable for.

If this delivery inertia is not addressed quickly, the leader could quite easily spiral into a situation where they look outwardly capable and confident of delivery but struggle internally to break free of the grip of fear. At this point, leaders start to look for ways to shift accountability for the said work on to other persons or other teams.

As an Emerging Leader, you must be clear about what you know – and how valuable your knowledge is. You must see yourself first as a carrier of solutions – and back your knowledge to be useful when required. At the same time, you must be clear about where the gaps in your knowledge, ability or experience exist. With regards to the gaps you identify, it is important that you do not define yourself by them but use the knowledge of them as opportunities to learn and get better at what you do. This approach will enable you to accept accountability for stretch tasks when such opportunities present themselves.

Lack of Confidence – this is yet another common root cause of accountability failure. Although closely related to the fear of stretch challenges, the lack of confidence could be a more damaging barrier. Leaders typically have a sense of accountability that feeds off the confidence placed in them by clients, who are expectant of a level of service delivery, subordinates who are expectant of a level of direction, peers who are expectant of a level of collaboration or their senior management who are expectant of a level of support. This confidence helps the leader put her best performance forward and is the impetus that drives excellent delivery.

As an Emerging Leader, it is always a great positive when you know that your clients, peers, managers and team members have faith or confidence in something that you have. Whether the faith they have is in your ability to deliver, or your attitude to work or even your experience in certain situations– it really does not matter. What does matter is that you are valued. A person who feels valued is better placed to step up and take on the mantle –

and pressures – of accountability for delivery. By the same token, a person who feels more tolerated than valued will most likely be reluctant to take up accountability for task delivery.

It is pertinent to note here, that over and above the confidence placed in you by those around you, it is the confidence that comes from within you that has the greatest potency to affect your development as an Emerging Leader. Regardless of who professes you to be the greatest they have ever seen; it is important that you believe in the qualities that you have within you. It is also vital that this belief is well managed such that it does not spill over into arrogance. That said, your self-confidence is key to your inclination to assume accountability for your actions and for the results of the work you do. When a leader has low levels [or is completely devoid] of self-confidence, they fall into a self-preservation mode shielding themselves from accepting accountability for tasks or actions.

In conclusion, accountability is the invisible trait that manifests as a visible impact on the delivery levels that an Emerging Leader can produce. Leaders who will leave a mark in the sands of time are those who will overcome many obstacles to seize the mantle of accountability. These are the leaders who are not afraid of failure. These are the leaders who are not afraid to be ridiculed by friends and foes. These leaders serve their teams and communities with distinction because they are willing to sacrifice themselves in order to get work done – and should the work not get done as expected, will still step forward and be accountable for the fallout. They are the Emerging Leaders who have emerged to stay. I ask myself many times if I am one of them.

<u>Examine – Equip - Emerge</u>

Some questions on accountability you will need to ask yourself as you continually emerge into your area of leadership include:

<u>Accountability</u>

1. The challenge of accountability affects Emerging Leaders in different ways. How do you handle this challenge?

   ....
   ....
   ....
   ....
   ....

2. Accountability drives a leader to take ownership of actions taken – as well as any consequence of those actions [whether positive or negative]. How have you dealt with mistakes you have made as a leader?

   ....
   ....
   ....
   ....
   ....

3. Effective leadership and accountability are inseparable – you cannot have one without the other. List some personal examples [or examples from other leaders] where accountability has led to effective delivery of value.

   ....

....

....

....

....

4. Self-assessment is a key component of accountability, enabling the Emerging Leader to continuously improve delivery levels. How have you objectively analysed failures such that your next delivery has improved on the last one?

....

....

....

....

....

..

5. How do you repay trust placed in you by leaders, peers and clients?

....

....

....

....

....

6. What is your understanding of the relationship between individual accountability and team / organizational accountability?

....

....

....
....
....

7. When faced with a stretch challenges, leaders can be susceptible to "delivery inertia" – finding it difficult to deliver on a task they already accepted accountability for. How would you as an Emerging Leader deal with this situation?

....
....
....
....
....

8. What is your understanding of the relationship between self-confidence and accountability? How has confidence in your ability helped you in the past to deliver results?

....
....
....
....
....

Accountability is the measure of a leader's height.
- Jeffrey Benjamin

chapter 10

Selfless Service Mindset

Earn your success based on service to others, not at the expense of others.
- H. Jackson Brown, Jr.

O f the thousands of definitions that exist for leadership, a great many of them agree that leaders are people who exert influence. These definitions are worded differently and many have a series of qualifiers to differentiate them from other definitions. I am – as I have already mentioned in this book – a student of leadership and in all of my studying, I have come to understand that there is a noble trait that binds all great leaders together – they all serve [or served] something to humanity. For clarity, I must state that despots, tyrants, dictators and all persons of questionable character that the world sometimes miscategorises as "leaders" are exempted from my definition of "leader". Service is the noble heart of leadership, and is only displayed by the men and women whose hearts minds and souls are [or were] committed to the improvement of the lot of humanity. All leaders are servants – therefore as an Emerging Leader, you must inquire of yourself, "what am I serving humanity with?"

To help with the answers that you could come up with, we should step back and ask how we define the concept of "service". I will put forward the definition that I have used in my personal journey of leadership and also in teaching leaders across the world. "*Service is the selfless deployment of ability, skill, capacity knowledge or resources with the express aim of solving problems for or adding value to a beneficiary other than self*".

> **Selflessness is at the very core of service, and Emerging Leaders should never forget this.**

There are some key words and phrases to note in this definition – the first being "**selfless**". As an Emerging Leader, if you want to produce the levels of service that will truly impact your world, you must be prepared to serve without consideration for self. Service must truly be unselfish and must carry at its heart the desire to make someone or something better than its pre-service state. The speech given by President J. F. Kennedy has been referred to repeatedly and its sentiments still ring true – especially if you aspire to the full discovery and deployment of your leadership potential. It is so much more beneficial for you to think of what you can do for your clients, community or country – than to think of what they can do for you. Selflessness is at the very core of service, and Emerging Leaders should never forget this. Many years ago, I listened to a veteran entrepreneur tell a small group about the reasons for his success. One of the things that stood out for me was his assertion that he never went into any venture looking for financial benefits – rather, he went in looking to use whatever skill, ability, experience and time resources that he had to solve an identified problem.

> **Rather, he went in looking to use whatever skill, ability, experience and time resources that he had to solve an identified problem.**

The second key word in the definition of service is "**deployment**". It is important to note for all Emerging Leaders that the idea of service is not the same as the experience of service. As it is often said, "the proof of the pudding is in the eating", service is only considered complete when a deployment takes place. If you are a leader in government, this is a particularly pertinent point. The political "sector" is well known for the production of promises, manifestos and blueprints. In the chase for the voter's endorsement, politicians are typically keen to paint a picture of the future that shows the best possible outcomes from them – and the worst possible outcomes from the opponents. However, history tells us that politicians [regardless of whether the promises were made in good faith or were "beefed up" to deliberately mislead] typically struggle to convert the promise of service into the reality of service. As an Emerging Leader, you must set your heart to deliver on the promises of service that you make. It is much better not to make a promise than to make one and fail to deliver. The integrity of a leader is in danger of sliding downwards with every service promised that is not delivered. This is why it is important to deploy all that you have in the drive to deliver the service that you promise.

The key phrase in the definition of service is "*solving problems or adding value*". This relates to the motive of service. As an Emerging Leader, you must be clear about your motive for doing anything. If you create or support a service, you must ensure that the service provides a solution to a problem or adds value to the recipient of that service. If neither of these happen, you are better off not taking part in that activity.

THE MOST IMPORTANT PERSON IN SERVICE DELIVERY

Conventional service delivery wisdom has told us over the years that the customer or client who receives the service is the most important personality in the service provision and service delivery equation. Service, as we have learnt

> **It is quite important to be aware of your strengths as a service provider**

involves doing something to benefit another. This understanding has driven the age-old service mantra "the customer is always right". The birth of the "customer-centric" service movement is predicated on this understanding. Therefore, as long as the person being served is happy with the results, we can assume that good service has been delivered.

I would like to be fair and state that this approach has got a lot going for it and it does have some success stories. I do see however, a tendency of this approach to groom the service deliverer into a well-oiled tool or machine that is primed to provide the best possible reaction or solution to the customer. This is in my experience, a "reactive service" model. My experience of service delivery as a provider as well as a customer tells me that this is not entirely accurate. My study of the theory and practicalities of service delivery has persuaded me to think differently, and as such put it forward that the servant (the person who delivers the service) and not the customer, is the most important personality in the service delivery equation.

In order to get excellent service delivered and experienced, there is a need to focus more on the person of the service provider than on the skills they possess or have been taught to use. When the focus is on the skill set, we are limited to the customer's view of how well the skills work. The service provider is also concerned with how well the training received has worked in the provision of service. On the other hand, when the person of the service provider is the focus, the service equation becomes more about giving than receiving. The issue is no longer about trying to match up with the demands [or even the idiosyncrasies] of the customer, but proactively looking at how the mind of the service provider works – regardless of who the customer is, how difficult the customer may be or how "important" a particular customer might be. The more we know about the service provider, the more we know what levels of service can possibly be delivered. Better still, the more a service provider knows about himself, the better he is able to give of himself to meeting the customer's needs.

> **The impact you will have on your world is a function of who you are and what your mind produces. These two baselines are the launch pads for everything you do as a leader.**

As an Emerging Leader therefore, it is quite important to be aware of your strengths as a service provider – to ask yourself some searching questions about your character.

- Why do you want to serve?
- Why do you want to serve in this particular arena?
- How resilient are you under the pressure of delivery, schedule and quality?

- How important is the quality of delivery to you?
- What are you willing to give in service that is over and above the template defined by the service manual?
- Under which conditions would you possibly be unable to serve your best?
- What is your best service?

Your honest answers to these and other similar questions will define the quality of service that any customer should reasonably expect from you. Your character as a servant is the key driver of service capacity. The collective character of a service department is the key driver of a service culture in an organisation. When service becomes a thing of personal significance to the servant, the most productive and most satisfactory service is released by the servant – and experienced by the customer. This brings me to my "other" but still quite relevant definition of service: "*Service is about understanding your significance to your work, team, organisation or business – and making a personal commitment that obliges you to selflessly deploy that significance in adding value to others.*"

As an Emerging Leader, you may be curious as to just what your "significance" is to your organisation or to the people around you. I will point you to the variety of functions in which you may be expected to operate in any role that provides service. I have grown as a servant myself to understand these functions of my service. You may also have seen yourself operate within your organisation as a supporter,

> **Observable behaviour provides a mirror to your character as a person – this is because every external action is born of internal thought.**

sounding board, reference point, example, knowledge-fountain, change-maker, guide, helper, leader, enabler, encourager, supplier, peacemaker, pacemaker, facilitator or champion. This list is not exhaustive, but shows just how important the servant is to the whole discussion about service.

> Your character is the foundation on which your ability to produce excellent service will be built.

THE MINDSET OF AN EFFECTIVE SERVICE PROVIDER

As an Emerging Leader, the impact you will have on your world is a function of who you are and what your mind produces. These two baselines are the launch pads for everything you do as a leader. Ideas generated from the mind are known to be the greatest product of humanity. When a leader is adjudged to have had either a positive or negative impact – it is simply the case that the product of that leader's mind has been assessed and assigned a score. Service, like all things leaders provide, is therefore more about the mind of the leader than the physical manifestation of the

> As President Abraham Lincoln once said "Nearly all men can stand adversity, but if you want to test a man's character, give him power"

service. Many programmes have tried to improve service delivery by focusing on fixing the way a service professional smiles, the number of rings in which a call must be answered or even the dress code defined for the office environment – all important items but not as important as understanding how the mind of the servant works. As long as you can find the origin of and motivation for service in your mind – and your motives are right, you can be confident that your place as an excellent service provider is assured. My study of service delivery has enabled me to identify four key constructs of the mind of the service provider.

> **Committed leaders are those who do not quit when the going gets tough, they are those who rub their hands with glee at the prospect of facing a new challenge**

1. PASSION

This is an internally driven force that provides the focus, dynamism and direction, which differentiates real leaders from the hordes of floaters and bystanders that lay claim to leadership. The passion for service is not something that can be taught. It is akin to a form of energy that can be harnessed. As an Emerging Leader, you must be passionate about serving, excited by opportunities to serve and driven by a passion to see the best results delivered for the recipients of your service. In the event that you come up against difficulties, your passion will have the power to strengthen your resolve and keep you focused on solution delivery. Truly great service can only be delivered by leaders with great passion. I have often been asked what the "passion to serve" looks like. If that question comes to you, simply think of the one thing that does not work in the way you would like it to – the one thing you wish you had the power to change. The hunger for that change sometimes manifests as an on-going ache [or sometimes, a feeling of resentment for those not in a position to effect a change]. The hunger for change is what translates into the passion for service.

2. VISION

This is the indispensable ability of a servant to "see" the end result of the delivered service from the beginning. As an Emerging Leader, it is important that you have a clear vision of the service you deliver. You must determine within yourself to deliver excellence even before you start the service delivery. A vision of excellent delivery will help you unleash from within yourself, the desire, dedication and discipline that you require. Your vision for service will also provoke your powers of innovation and creativity – enabling you to take your service delivery beyond the ordinarily expected levels into the realms of the unexpected and extraordinary. Vision will also expand your awareness of potential and give you the courage to challenge existing service delivery models. When you serve with vision, you will be uncomfortable with anything that is less than the excellence you have "seen" in your mind. Some of the great servants that I have read about – such as Mohandas Gandhi and Mother Teresa have shown how the vision in the heart of a leader moves them to provide excellent service and leadership. As a visionary servant, you need to have lived in the reality of the solution from the clients' viewpoint, thereby making the excellence of the result a personal drive – this way of serving can influence those who work with you and cause them to produce better results than expected. The Emerging Leader who serves with vision is usually a few steps "ahead of the game" – much like the chess grand master who thinks several moves ahead of the current board situation. As Wayne

Gretzky once said, "A good hockey player plays where the puck is, a great hockey player plays where the puck will be".

3. CHARACTER

Character is the unique and inherent complex of all the behavioural, emotional and mental attributes that govern the moral qualities and ethical standards of a person in any situation. Effectively, your character defines the core principles that you live by – informing a code of conduct that controls your thought processes, actions, reactions and decisions. As an Emerging Leader, observable behaviour provides a mirror to your character as a person – this is because every external action is born of internal thought [you cannot produce seen actions that do not come from your unseen thoughts].

Your character is the foundation on which your ability to produce excellent service will be built. In the same way as it is impossible to build a useful building on an inadequate foundation, it is impossible for you as an Emerging Leader to deliver excellent service on a shady character. The first thing that must be examined when preparing yourself for a life of service is the solidity of your character. Are you who you say you are? What core values do you hold as true? What tests have you passed through by the strength of your character? What weaknesses do you have that you are aware of, acknowledge and are working to fix? What strengths – forged through character building – do you bring to the place of service?

Without a sound character, leaders, tend to be servants of their own convenience – and not true servants. If you read or hear of leaders who have failed in the political arena – creating and bequeathing failed states to their people – you have read or heard of a deficiency in character, which translates to a variety of failures in service delivery. As President Abraham Lincoln once said *"Nearly all men can stand adversity, but if you want to test a man's character, give him power"*. Always remember that as an Emerging Leader, you cannot possibly serve out better results than your character dictates.

4.   COMMITMENT

This is the unshakeable dedication to a cause, goal or vision. Commitment is that component of the servant's mindset that makes the place of service less of a burden and more of a blessing to the servant. By extension, the committed servant is a blessing to the client - as this commitment drives them to push beyond the expectations of their natural abilities. Commitment is a crucial leadership attitude that all Emerging Leaders should cultivate, as it will be required through every step of their journeys as leaders.

Committed leaders are those who do not quit when the going gets tough, they are those who rub their hands with glee at the prospect of facing a new challenge, they are those whose mind is made up to stick with their delivery of a solution regardless of the pain that the road to that solution brings. As an Emerging Leader, your great vision, powerful sense of purpose, great ability, substantial subject-matter expertise and effective communication ability must be complemented by a fierce commitment to serving out the solution that you have to deliver. This commitment is one of the building blocks of the winning attitude that can be seen as a common trait of great leaders who served successfully.

It is important to note that an Emerging Leader's commitment to service must not be driven by the promise of personal reward or recognition, rather it must be driven first by a strong desire to see the completion of solution delivery and then by the satisfaction that the end user or client will derive from experiencing the solution. The greatest leaders of the past and current generations are those who gave – or are giving – themselves in order to make something better for others. This is the spirit of service that defines the type of leader our world needs today in all spheres of life – to bring the required solutions within the political, educational, military, health, spiritual and financial systems.

In summary, it is pertinent to note the change in the mindset of the "typical" service recipient. Several studies have shown that the recipients of service [clients, customers etc.] have become much more demanding, discerning, aggressive, impatient, knowledgeable, persistent and observant than they were 50 years ago. This is one key reason that necessitates the emergence of a new breed of servant – more knowledgeable, more committed, more passionate, more integrated in character, more perceptive, more understanding, more compassionate, stronger and more durable than ever before.

Examine – Equip - Emerge

Selfless Service Mind Set - Chapter 10

1. In order to get excellent service delivered and experienced, there is a need to focus more on the person rather than the skills of the service provider. Do you agree with this? Please state reasons for the position you have taken on this statement.

   ....
   ....
   ....
   ....
   ....

2. What strengths do you have as an Emerging Leader providing a service?

   ....
   ....
   ....
   ....
   ....

3. What areas do you need to improve upon as an Emerging Leader providing a service?

   ....
   ....
   ....
   ....

4. What are you most passionate about – that you would give up anything to be a part of the solution?

....

....

....

....

5. Today's customer is quite enlightened, discerning, demanding and can be fussy about service quality. This requires the service of a particularly well-rounder service provider. As an Emerging Leader, how would you face up to the challenge of today's service recipients?

....

....

....

....

....

6. What is your understanding of the relationship between passion and service delivery?

....

....

....

....

....

7. What is your understanding of the relationship between vision and service delivery?

....

....

....
....
....

8. What is your understanding of the relationship between character and service delivery?

....
....
....
....
....

9. What is your understanding of the relationship between commitment and service delivery?

....
....
....
....
....

I think leadership is service and there is power in that giving: to help people, to inspire and motivate them to reach their fullest potential.
Denise Morrison

Closing Statements

For many decades, leaders have been held back from emerging by an accepted understanding that you emerge once into leadership – coming through as a young person [either in school, college, university or through apprenticeships and early entrepreneurism activity]. This myopic view of leadership emergence is still prevalent today in 2016 – and forms the basis of many multi-billion-pound learning programmes put forward by governments, educational institutions and respected scholars in the developed and developing world.

This is one of the key barriers that this book seeks to break, thereby enabling you the reader to understand that you can emerge into your own leadership space daily as the sun rises – or even multiple times in a single day. As an Emerging Leader, what counts is not the time of the day or the so-called "period" of your life. Your whole existence has always had a purpose attached to it. The world you live in lacked something specific before your arrival – something that you are uniquely designed and empowered to deliver and actualize. You do need to understand and accept this as a starting point to your continued emergence and relevance as a leader. My submission on this particularly important issue is that you are a leader – whether you have previously realized this or not. You may be a leader in waiting, in

> **You can emerge into your own leadership space daily as the sun rises – or even multiple times in a single day.**

the process of first emergence, a leader in continued emergence or a leader currently in some form of hiatus. You may also a leader in danger of stagnation through inactivity, a leader under pressure of challenges or a leader on the way back from a period of dormancy. The fact remains that you are a leader, and the characteristics written about in this book apply to you.

I have heard it said quite often that nothing teaches better than experience. There are times in the life of an Emerging Leader when it will become clear that one or more of the options selected are the wrong ones. For some, it may be the decision to invest in a particular opportunity or to enter into an agreement with a partner. For others it may be the decision to take no action, where positive action would have been the way to go. Some leaders will experience this in private, family-related matters. Whatever the case may be, a point will be reached when the leader must decide whether to continue in the hope and expectation of a turn around, or accept that the option taken was the wrong one – and hence seek a new direction. Whenever you get to a crossroads of this nature, your understanding of these characteristics discussed in this book will be of great help in your decision making process.

The principles discussed in this book will hold true for leaders young and old, male and female from any nation regardless of the level of development of such nations. This is because these principles embedded in the characteristics are not subject to change based on any of the aforementioned categorisations. As an Emerging Leader, you will find that some of these characteristics are your identifiable strengths. And so, you will observe that you are not particularly strong in following the principles that underpin some of the other characteristics. The key to becoming the effective Emerging Leader that you want to be is in ensuring that you build positively on your areas of strength and work hard to minimise the effects of your weak areas – turning them into strengths as time and experience goes by.

In closing, I submit – just as the various chapters of this book have laid out, that the Emerging Leader is more than any individual attribute possessed, more than any individual behaviour or attitude, more than the solution to a particular problem and more than the expectations of senior management, peers and team members. The Emerging Leader is a complex mix of the aforementioned coupled with a special sprinkling of "stardust" – built into his DNA [specifically designed as a consequence of purpose].

Bibliography

- **Schumpeter J.** (1942), "Capitalism, Socialism, and Democracy", Harper, New York
- **Joanna Barsh, Marla M. Capozzi, and Jonathan Davidson** (2008), "Leadership Innovation", McKinsey Quarterly,
- **Carson, Clayborne and Shepard, Kris (editors). (2001)** "A Call to Conscience: The Landmark Speeches of Dr. Martin Luther King, Jr." New York: Warner Books
- *Arthur Farstad (Ed), The Holy Bible,* New King James Version. Nashville: HarperCollins
- **Pinder, Richard (2013);** "Leadership Transition: Essential Elements and Pitfalls of Leadership Change" One Rib Publications
- **Maxwell, John C. (1999);** "The 21 Indispensable Qualities of a Leader"; Thomas Nelson
- **Munroe, Myles (2014);**" The Power of Character in Leadership: How Values, Morals, Ethics and Principles Affect Leaders"; Whittaker House
- **Pinder Richard (2013);** "Integrity, the Vital Leadership Quality"; One Rib Publications
- **Green,Andy (2008);** "Effective Personal Communication Skills for Public Relations"; Page India Private Limited
- **Templar, Richard (2005);** "The Rules of Management"; Pearson Power
- **Covey, Stephen P. (1990),** "Principle Centered Leadership"; Simon and Schuster UK
- ESPN Staff, espnfc.com.au, 2015. *"Real Betis' Rafael van der Vaart: Leaving Tottenham was stupid"* [online] Available at: http://www.espnfc.com.au/barclays-premier-league/story/2531486/rafael-van-der-vaart-leaving-spurs-my-most-stupid-decision [Accessed 12 October 2015].
- Wendy Zellner, Stephanie Anderson Forest et al, Bloomberg.com, 2001. *"The Fall of Enron: How ex-CEO Jeff Skilling's strategy grew so complex that even his boss couldn't get a handle on it"* [online] Available at: http://www.bloomberg.com/news/articles/2001-12-16/the-fall-of-enron, [Accessed 22 August 2015].
- Jacquelyn Smith, ukbusinessinsider.com, 2016. *"Mark Cuban, Kobe Bryant, and 15 other people whose incredible work ethic paid off"* [online] Available at: http://uk.businessinsider.com/hard-working-successful-people-2016-4?r=US&IR=T, [Accessed 09 April 2016]

Images links

Chapter 1.
www.globaldigitalcitizen.org

Chapter 2.
www.activerain.com

Chapter 3.
www.fierceinc.com

Chapter 4.
www.youthensnews.com

Chapter 5.
www.sandiegosatacttutoring.com

Chapter 6.
www.habrahabr.ru

Chapter 7.
www.dreamstime.com

Chapter 8.
www.dreamstime.com

Chapter 9.
www.meanderingmind.us

Chapter 10.
www.highlanderdata.com

www.ingramcontent.com/pod-product-compliance
Lightning Source LLC
Chambersburg PA
CBHW060026210326
41520CB00009B/1018